Michigan Revealed

Exploring the Mitten's Thumb

Leslie Cieplechowicz

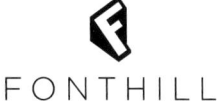

FONTHILL

Dedicated to my kids, Zachary, Hannah, Ingrid, and Isaac.
It's been a hell of a ride.

Fonthill Media Inc.
www.fonthillmedia.com
office@fonthillmedia.com

First published 2024

Copyright © Leslie Cieplechowicz 2024

ISBN 978-1-62545-131-6

Typeset in Gotham Book
Printed and bound in England

Contents

About the Author   **4**

Introduction   **5**

1   Northeast Region   **13**

2   Southeast Region   **35**

3   Northwest Region   **58**

4   Southwest Region   **79**

About the Author

Leslie Cieplechowicz is a photographer who developed her craft by working the streets of Detroit as a paramedic and shooting old, historical buildings she found on her runs. Her love of creating unique imagery led her across the state, then the United States, then globally, where she recently finished shooting in the country of Cuba, documenting its fascinating culture, friendly people, and expanse of classical architecture and vintage automobiles. Her prior works include *Detroit Revealed: A Different View of the Motor City* and inclusion in *The Drifter and Other Unusual Tales*. She currently works as an instructor after leaving the road and spreads her love of photography to her students. More of her images can be viewed at www.4amphotography.com and on Facebook and Instagram at 4amphotographydetroit.

Introduction

Darkness enveloped my car and heavy snowflakes swirled around it, illuminated by my headlights. As I pulled into my ice glazed, dirt driveway, I felt the heaviness of my job slowly bleed down out of my boots. I had just finished a twelve-hour shift that had turned into thirteen hours, as a Detroit Fire Department paramedic, and I was weary. The day had been long and grueling, and there had been too much death. The shift had ended with a multiple vehicle car crash, where my partner and I had pulled broken, bloody bodies flaked with shattered glass from twisted metal while our numbing hands fumbled in the ferocious cold.

I sat rooted in my seat, watching the snow dance and twirl, the outline of my 1850s farmhouse serving as a backdrop. No sounds pierced the storm, and my brow began to unfurrow. Though living in the country in a house that was purchased as a fixer upper was challenging at times, I could think of no other place I would rather call home.

I have lived the Michigan's Thumb for over twenty-five years and have raised four children in this area of farmland dotted by small villages. My small property of ten acres has housed many furry and feathered residents over the decades, from noisy, ruffled hens to loyal, fierce shepherds to surly, runaway hogs to woolly baby lambs who bounced their way through rainy springs.

Over the years, I have wandered all over the Thumb, chatted with the farmers, drank at the local dive bars, laughed with the residents, and drove through historic, tiny towns that were gone in a blink of an eye. The Thumb has a small town, earthy, country charm. It is a place to escape the roar of the city, to meander down the empty, hushed roads, a place to be able to mediate and reflect. In my book, I share my favorite places, ones I hope you will learn to love as much as I do and will revisit again and again. Come out and bask in the peace and loveliness of my home region.

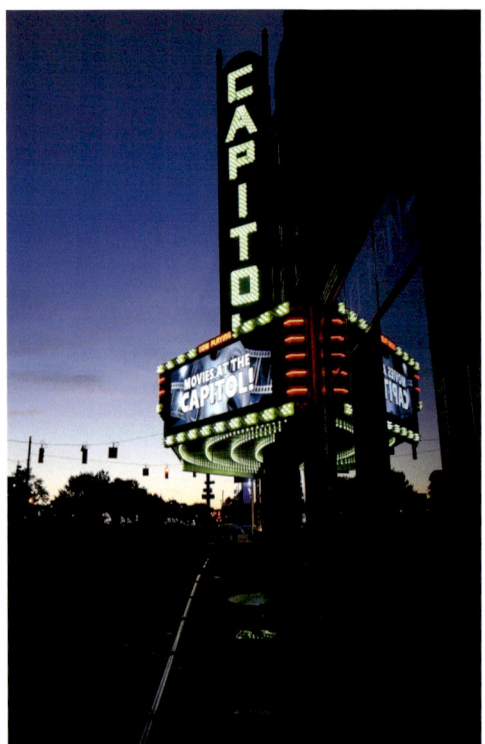

Left: The Capitol Theater beckoning to viewers with its humming neon letters.

Below: A girl relaxes next to her prize show cows at the Goodells 4-H Fair.

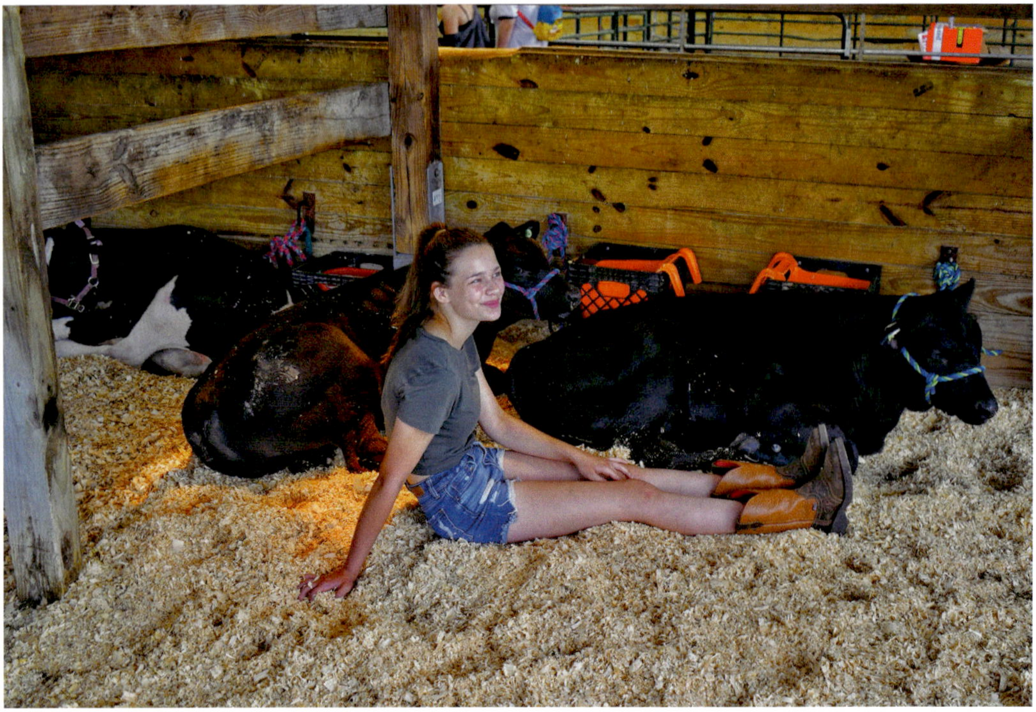

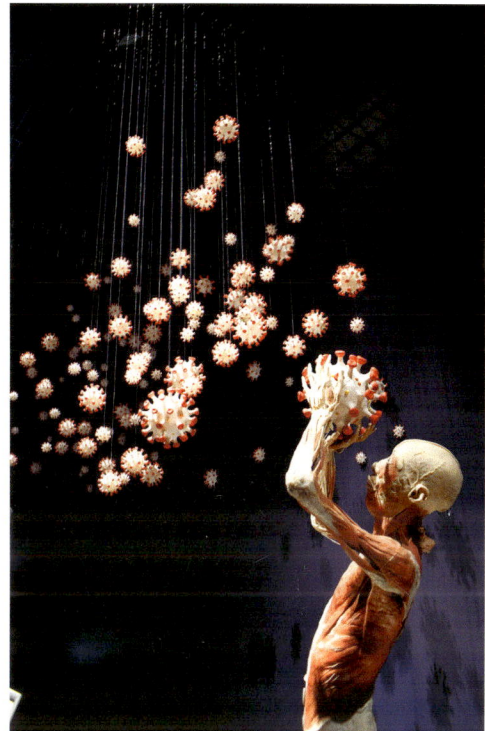

Right: Covid virus raining down on a figure at the Human Exhibit in the Sloan Museum in Flint.

Below: Lake Huron, during a bitter 4 degrees, sending its angry, icy waves crashing onto the shore.

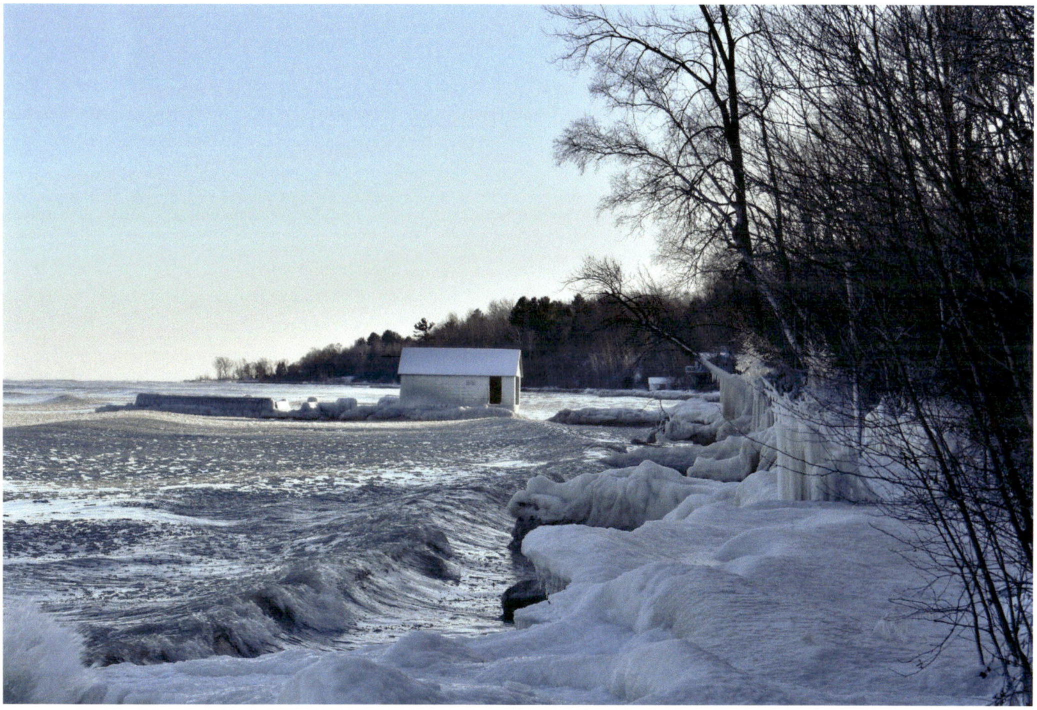

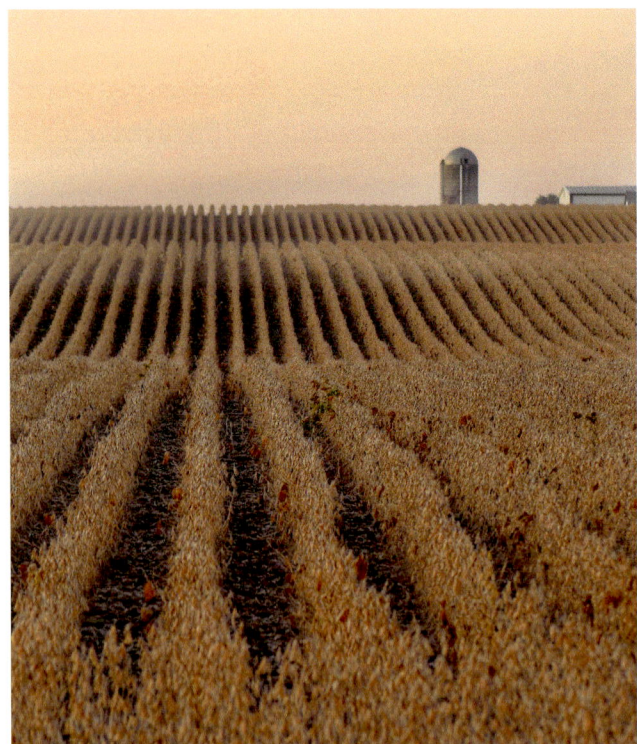

Left: A field of drying soybeans softly glowing under a salmon pastel autumn sky.

Below: The Black River in Port Huron, slipping into the St. Clair River as a gray wispy dawn greets it.

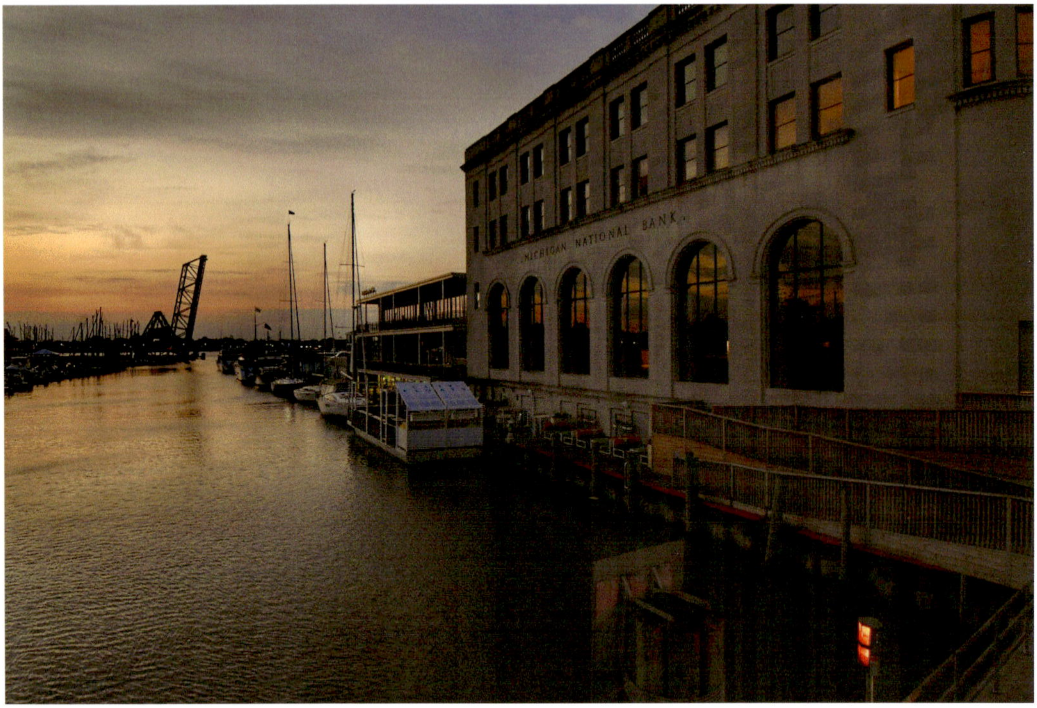

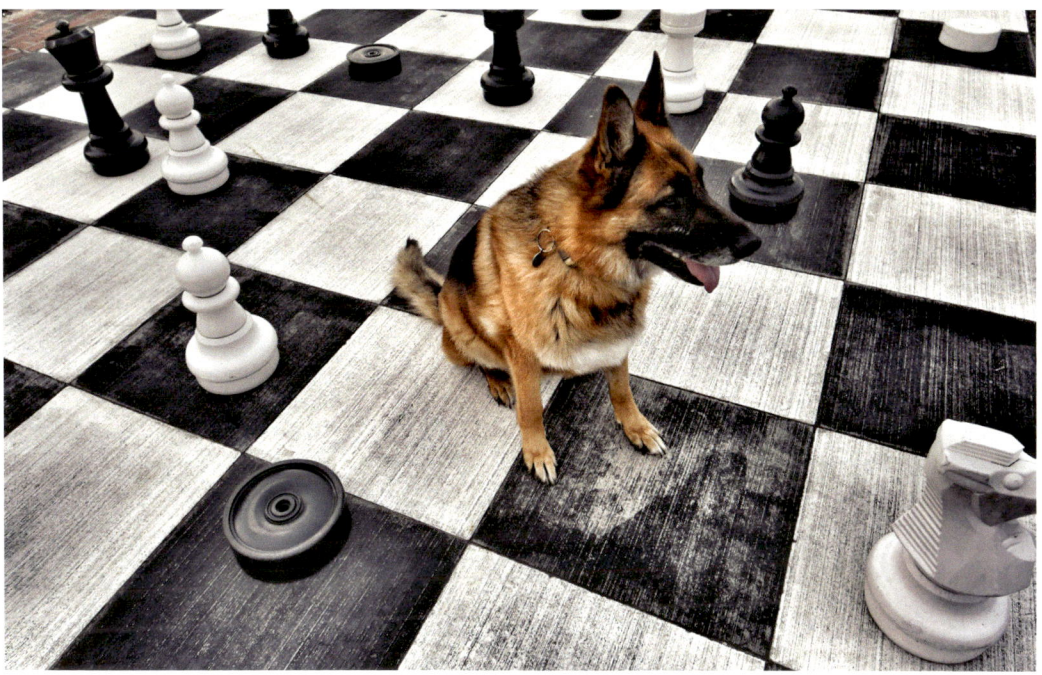

A German shepherd mimics a chess piece on the board in a park near the Fort Street Dock in Port Huron.

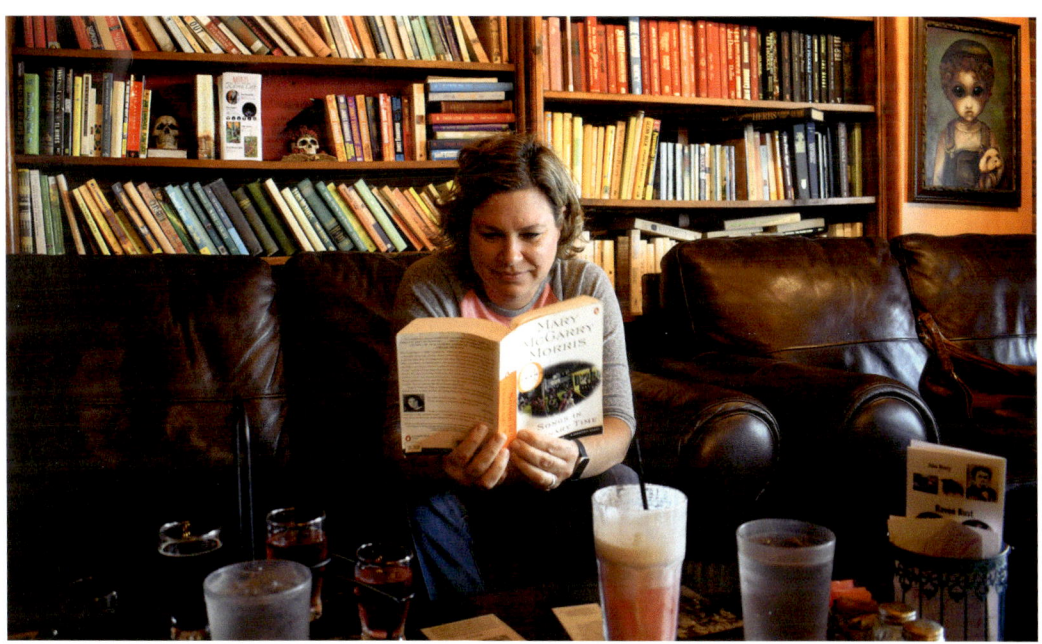

A woman enjoys a good read, surrounded by multiple tomes, at the funky coffeehouse, The Raven, in Port Huron.

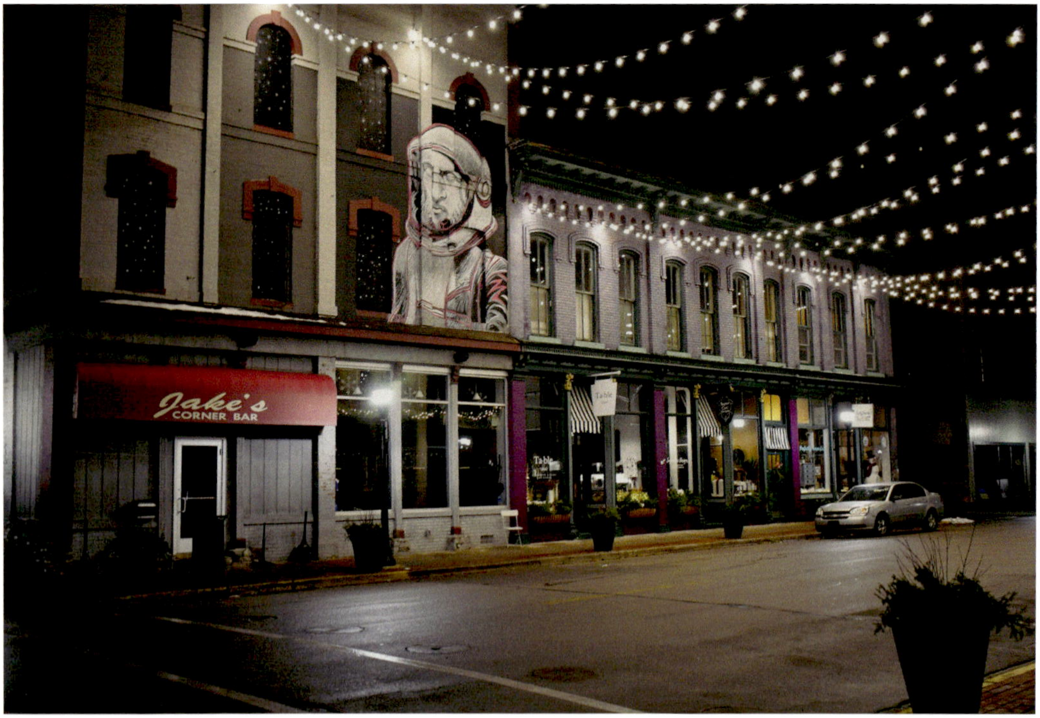

Above image: Downtown Bay City street scene with lights

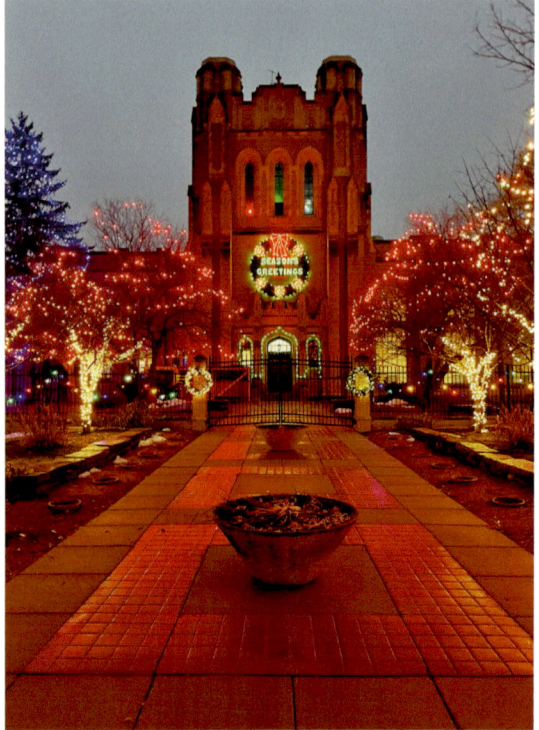

Above: Downtown Bay City under pale, gleaming lights.

Left: Saginaw Water Works decorated in its yearly bedazzling Christmas light display.

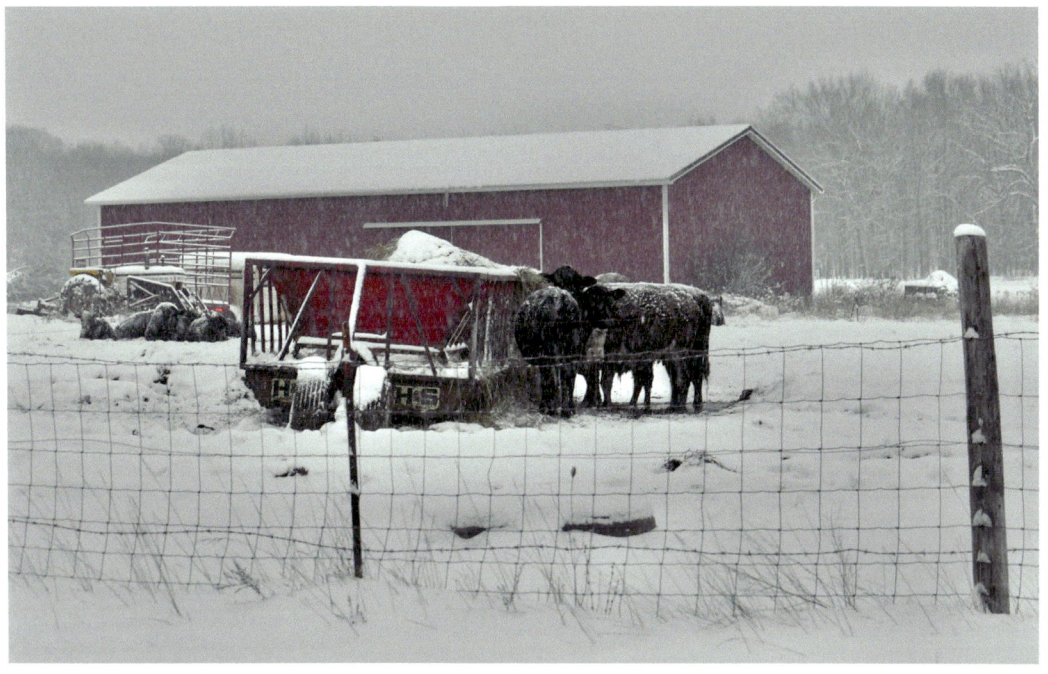

Cows sprinkled with snowflakes in Sanilac County.

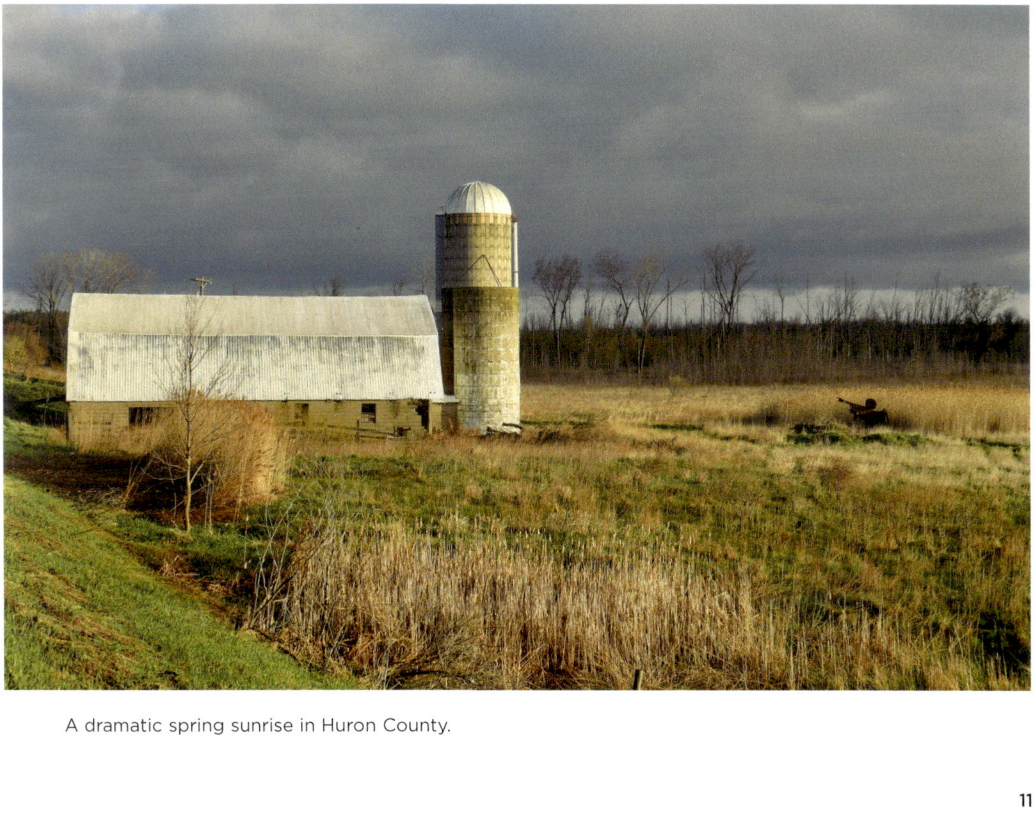

A dramatic spring sunrise in Huron County.

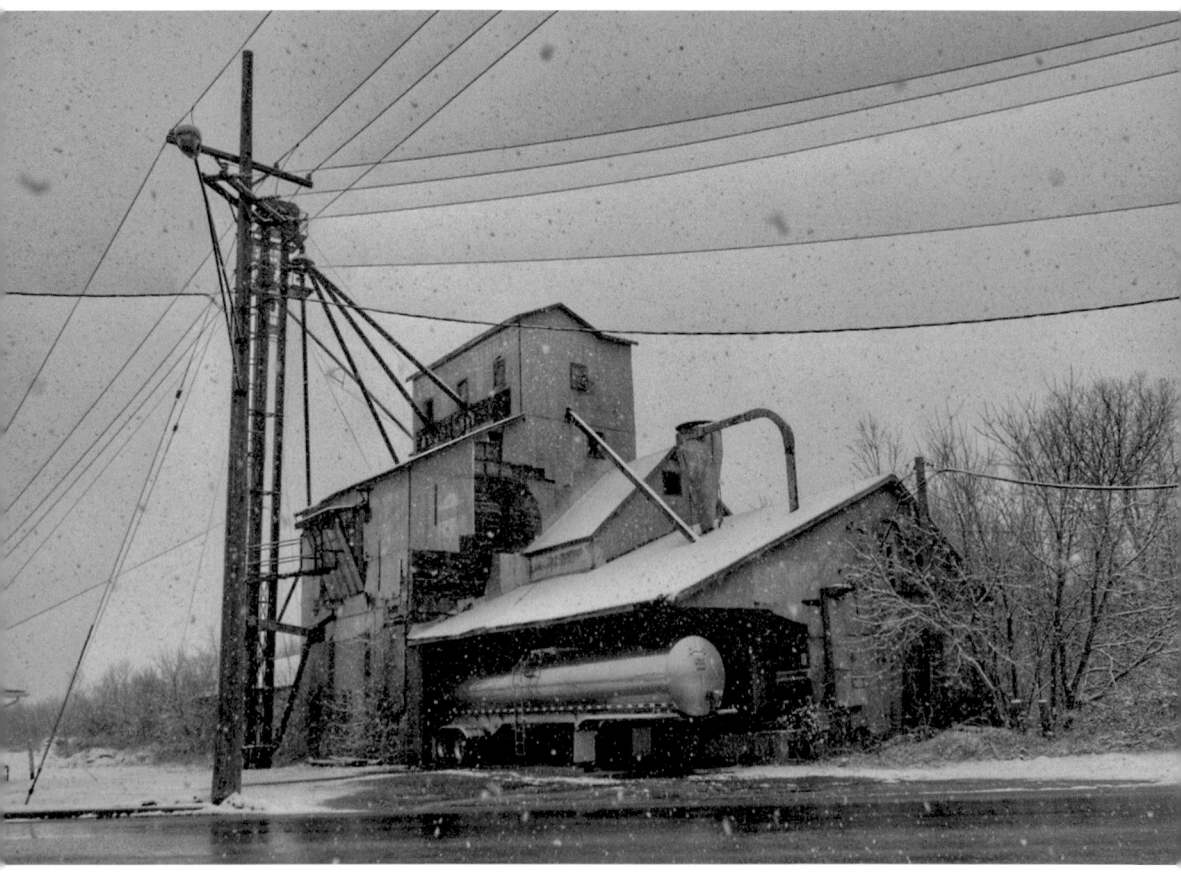

The old Avoca grain mill with snow wafting down, where farmers took their crops to be processed.

Northeast Region

Port Crescent State Park, at 1775 Port Austin Road in Port Austin, snuggles its golden dunes up to the vast, topaz blue Lake Huron. Its creamy, sandy shoreline is littered with fragments of bleached mussel shells. The beach is perfect for catching some warm rays or dipping toes into the refreshing lake. Wooden boardwalks lead you from the beach to a changing place with restrooms and to a platform where birds of prey soar, along with an identification key and a steel, circular statue silhouetting their forms in flight. At night, this same platform is a dark sky preserve, where twinkling stars and the shimmering Milky Way are splattered above. Trails snake throughout the park, perfect for a relaxing jaunt. The Pinnebog River ribbons through the area for five miles into Lake Huron and is perfect for kayaking. A kayak can be rented near the park at Tip-A-Thumb Kayak and Canoe Rental at 2475 Port Austin Road, Port Austin, or bring your own. An interesting tidbit of history is that the park rests on the site of the former lumber town Port Crescent, which met its demise when all the timber around the river basin was cut down in the 1880s.

Port Austin State Harbor at 8774 Lake Street, Port Austin, is at the very tip of Thumb and has a pier that extends into Lake Huron. Walk on its sturdy concrete and feel the spray of the lake kissing your cheeks. At the start of the pier is a pale, platinum beach if you want to dig your toes into the toasty sand or wade into the invigorating water. Across from the harbor is Bird Creek Park at 8746-8774 Lake Street, Port Austin, with an emerald grassy strip and a sandy shore for swimming. From both Port Austin State Harbor and Bird Creek Park, you can catch a glimpse of the Port Austin Reef Lighthouse standing two miles in the distance off the shore. Built in 1877, the lighthouse is perched on a rocky reef that is part of a network of treacherous ledges and rocky areas that stretch for 2.5 miles and have snagged many unknowing vessels. Experienced kayakers can paddle to the lighthouse for a closer look on a very calm day by renting a vessel from Port Austin Kayak, located at 119 E. Spring Street, Port Austin.

Sitting on 8685 Lake Street, Port Austin, is the charming boutique, The Cove, which showcases over fifty-five local artists from across Michigan and is run by artists. Colorful, whimsical sculptures adorn its front lawn, and the building is highlighted with cheerful turquoise siding. Inside, sunlight from a skylight make the art pieces glitter and shine. Peruse the many beautiful works in the shop, from unique jewelry to hand-crafted pottery to gorgeous paintings. Purchase gifts for all your family and friends while supporting local artists.

Turnip Rock, a rock formation that is one of Michigan's natural wonders, is located off the shore of Pointe Aux Barques. As the land area is private property, the only way to see Turnip Rock is by kayaking from Port Austin, along the Lake Huron shore. You can rent a kayak from Port Austin Kayak, located at 119 E. Spring Street, Port Austin. The seven-mile trip over shallow sparkling waters is a glorious way to explore the curving coastline. When you reach Turnip Rock, snap a few images of this geological formation formed over thousands of years.

After hiking and kayaking around the tip of the Thumb, enjoy a savory meal at the Tap Room at the Bird Creek Farms, at 282 Grindstone Road, Port Austin. The restaurant is part of a working 40-acre organic farm where many of its fresh ingredients come from. Try such sumptuous dishes as tenderloin steak bites, oysters on the half shell, pecan crusted salmon, and frog legs. To end the meal, top it off with a bucket of donuts doused with cream sauce.

Grindstone City has a compelling history about how the town was formed. In 1834, Captain Aaron G. Peer needed to take shelter while sailing Lake Huron in his schooner, the Rip Van Winkle, when a vicious storm engulfed it. He and his crew went ashore and found large, flat stones on the beach. Some of the rock was shipped to Detroit to pave a few streets near Jefferson Avenue and Woodward Avenue. Other stone was used to create foundations for buildings in Port Huron. As more sailors came to the area, they used the stones to sharpen their tools. In 1838, realizing the stone made excellent grindstones, Peer purchased land in the area and Grindstone City was born. Grindstone became world renowned for its stones until artificial carborundum caused the industry to collapse and created a ghost town. Today, a large, dated, two-ton grindstone marks what used to be a bustling town.

An old-fashioned general store is still in business, called Grindstone General Store, at 3206 Copeland Road, Port Austin, where local souvenirs stock the shelves. The store's claim to fame is its gigantic ice cream cones, filled with cold, frosty Stroh's ice cream, great to enjoy on a sizzling summer day while sitting on the shady porch.

Kernan Memorial Nature Sanctuary, located at the end of Pochart Road in Huron County next to Lake Huron, is a rustic area of sensitive wetlands, mud flats, and lonely beach stretched over 45 acres. A half-mile track wraps around Whiskey Harbor, which in the 1930s was a prime spot for bootlegging Canadian rum into the U.S. during Prohibition. In early March and November, the area is an excellent spot to see migratory shore birds who flourish in the shallow waters which discourage boaters. The secluded area can flood, making hiking wet, slippery, and muddy.

Sanilac Petroglyphs Historic State Park, at 8251 Germania Road, nestled near Cass City, displays early Native American carvings in sandstone that is hundreds of years old. The spirals, birds in flight, handprints, and other figures are teachings called *Ezhibiigaadek Asin*, meaning "written on stone," in the Anishinaabemowin language. Tribal groups have occupied the area for the past 8,000 years. For an interesting rendition of the history of the area and the carvings, take a tour with one of the knowledgeable park guides who will spin tales of yore about the carvings along with stories about the Great Thumb Fire of Michigan of 1881 which destroyed more than half the thumb region. After hearing lessons of the past, take a stroll along the dirt trail next to the whispering

Cass River and enjoy the beauty of the leafy, emerald forest creating a restful silence.

The Trescott Pier, located in Judge James H. Lincoln Memorial Park, at 1 Trescott Street, Harbor Beach, is a long pier extending 1,015 feet into Lake Huron. At its end, the Harbor Beach Lighthouse squats off in the distance. The pier's name gives a nod to Loren Trescott, the lighthouse keeper who from 1878 to 1912 kept ships safe. Glowing lights line the pier's sides while benches offer the perfect place to relax and listen to the rolling, foamy waves.

A two-story brick building sits at 105 N. Huron Avenue, Harbor Beach houses the Harbor Beach Area District Library and the Harbor Beach Community Theater. Underneath its arches is an ornate mural depicting shipwrecks, locomotives, agriculture, and Frank Murphy, the former Mayor of Detroit, Supreme Court Justice, and Governor of Michigan.

Want to learn more about Frank Murphy? Head to the Frank Murphy Memorial Museum at 142 S. Huron Avenue, Harbor Beach, located in a charming 1870s Victorian Gothic Revival house which was the birthplace of the former governor. The home also served as a *circa* 1880 law office. There are five buildings on the property, three of which can be toured. Immerse yourself in the history of this famous Michigander while viewing the beautiful, embroidered clothing and the multiple historic paintings. The museum also displays the largest collection of Philippine artifacts in the United States gifted to or purchased by Murphy when he served in the Philippines during 1933–1936 as Governor General after the country became a U.S. Commonwealth.

After exploring the city, enjoy Lake Huron up close by renting a kayak at Harbor Beach Kayak Rental, located at 1 Trescott Street, Harbor Beach. The sheltered harbor is great for beginners and sports such sites as the Harbor Beach Lighthouse perched on a rocky outcropping on the harbor's border, and skeletons of three shipwrecks, the *Dorcas Pendell*, the *George H. Waud*, and the *John Wesley*. The fascinating wrecks can be seen as you drift above them on calm, sunny days.

For a walk back into history, head to the Sanilac County Historic Village and Museum at 228 South Ridge Street, Port Sanilac. The village has over a dozen renovated vintage buildings to explore, including a general store with old fashioned penny candy, a working church, and a functioning centennial one-room schoolhouse. The ten acres also is planted with charming gardens filled with fragrant, colorful flowers. The 1872 Loop-Harrison mansion, furnished from the period, serves as the property's museum. Its collections include shipwreck relics, Native American pieces, and military memorabilia. An 1880s barn has been converted into a theater and hosts performances. Around Halloween, the village hosts a haunted Halloween Spook Walk, invoking the ghosts of the past. The village is a perfect place to explore the area's history with family and friends.

Lexington is a charming village lying next to the crystal blue Lake Huron, with a 108-slip harbor and a concrete path resting on rocks that shelter sandy shore. Stroll to the end of the pier and inhale the fresh breezy air while watching a crimson sunrise, then wander into the town with its quaint shops lining Main Street. The village hosts numerous events including a Christmas horse parade in December, where equestrians and their mounts are gaily dressed for the celebration, and the annual Bach Festival for lovers of classic music.

Swaying over the Black River in Croswell, in Riverbend Park at 39 Nims Street in Croswell, is the longest spanning suspension bridge in Michigan. The Michigan Sugar

Company constructed the bridge for the cost of $300 in 1905 so their factory workers could get across the Black River more easily. The bridge bounces and bucks as people walk over it, and at its park end entrance, a sign boldly states, "Be Good to Your Mother-in-Law." A festival celebrates the bridge every year in August and includes a cardboard boat race on the river.

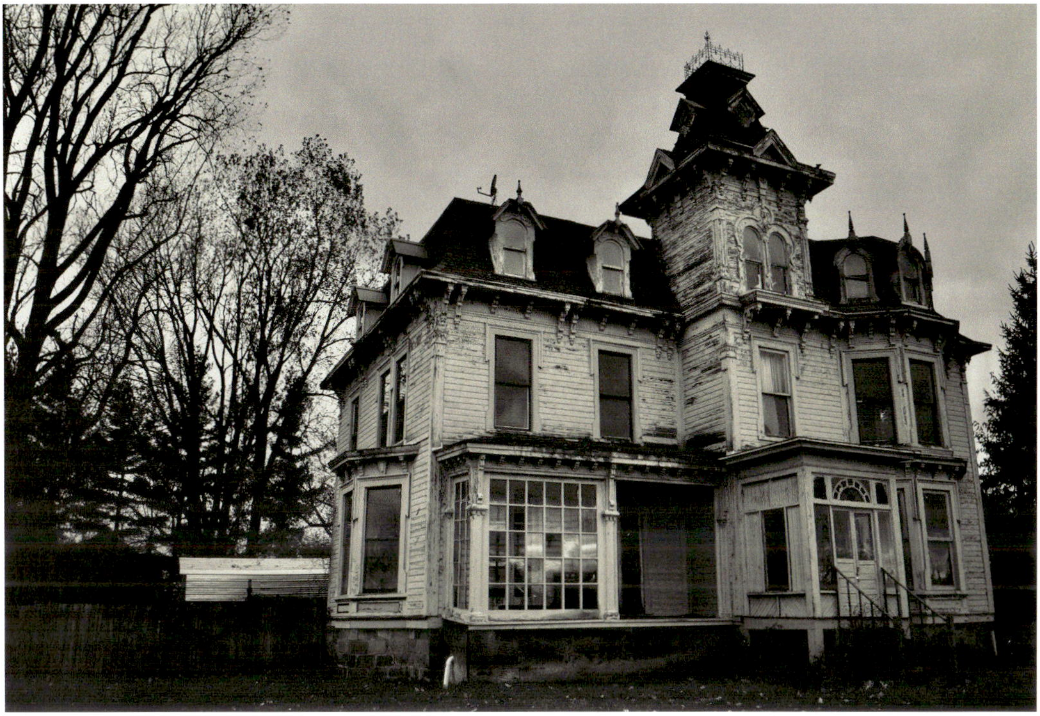

Above: A Victorian mansion brooding north of Brown City, which once hosted haunted tours.

Right: Port Austin Lighthouse perched in Lake Huron two miles off the coast.

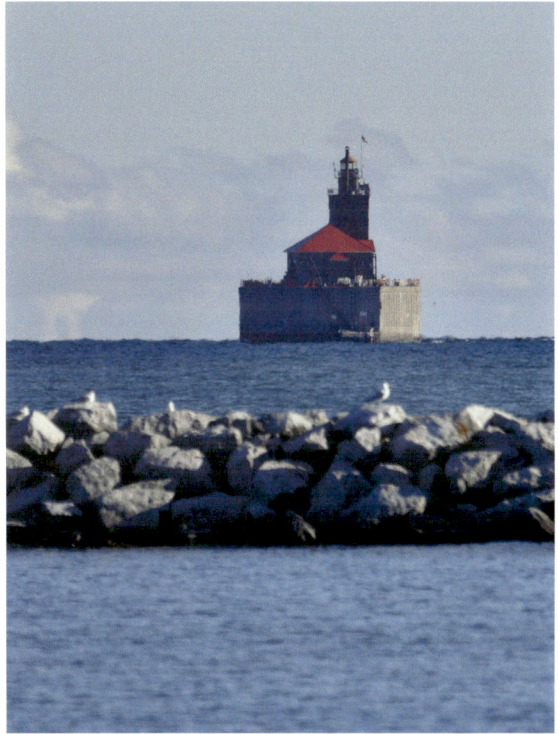

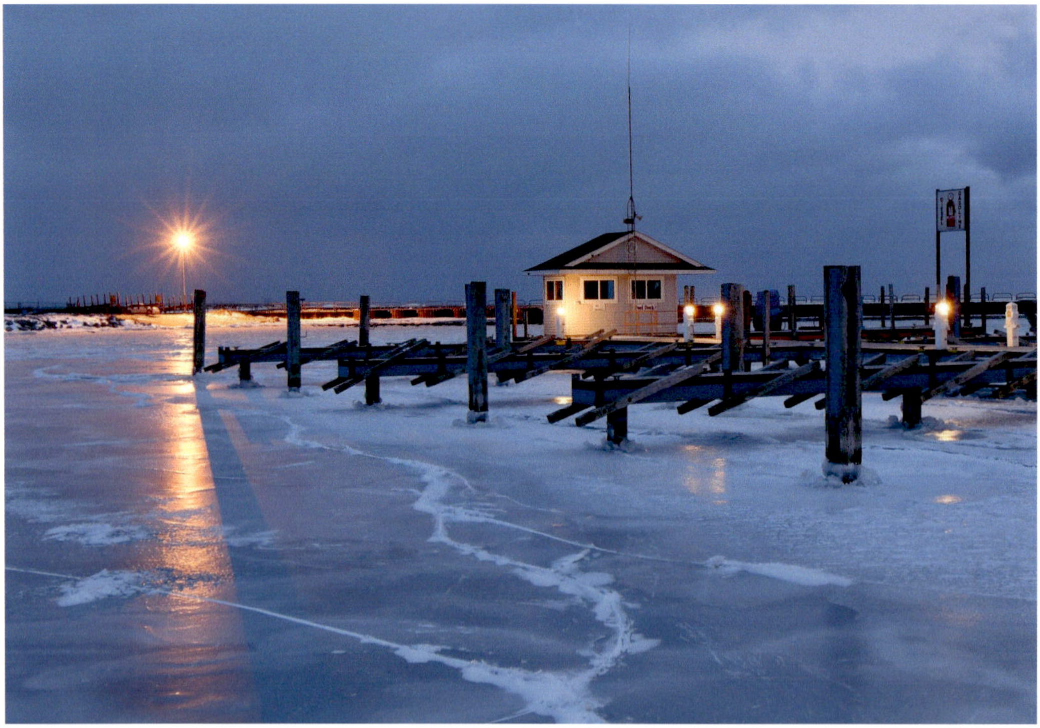

Port Sanilac Harbor silenced by a bitter cold that turned its waters into shimmering blue glass.

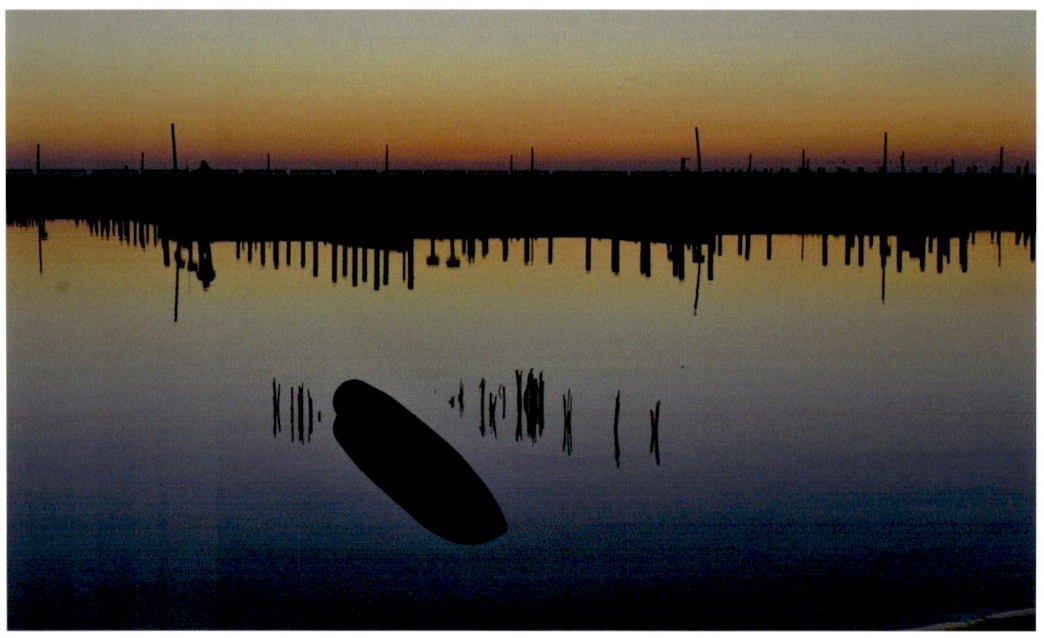

Lexington Harbor at sunrise, an abstract painting with tangerine and gray.

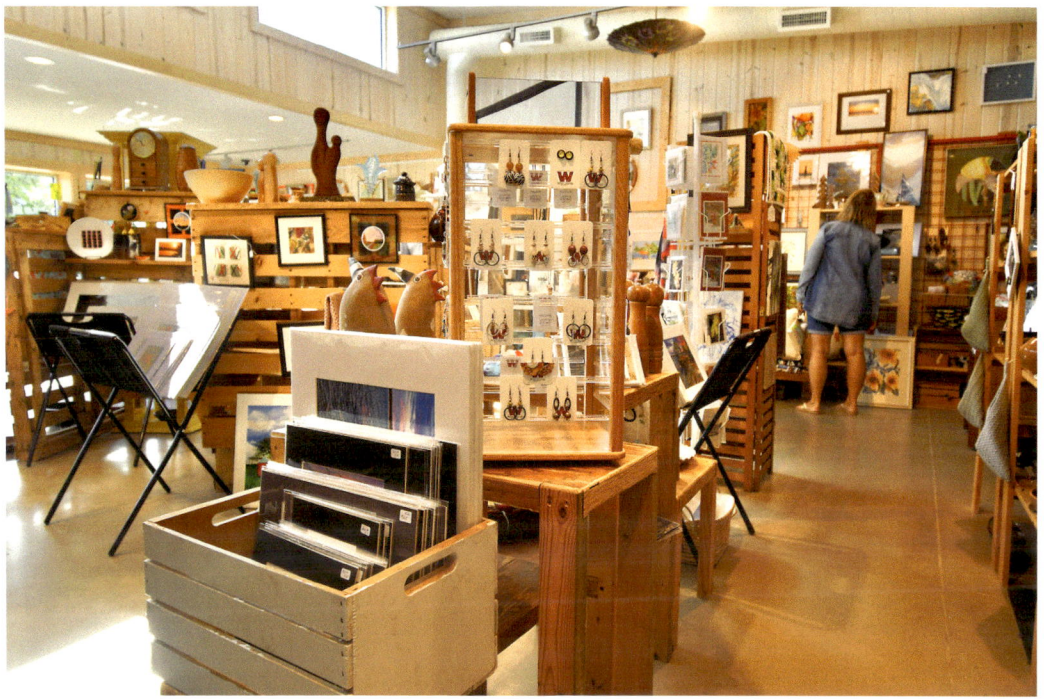

The charming interior of The Cove, a gallery in Port Austin for Michigan artists to display their creations.

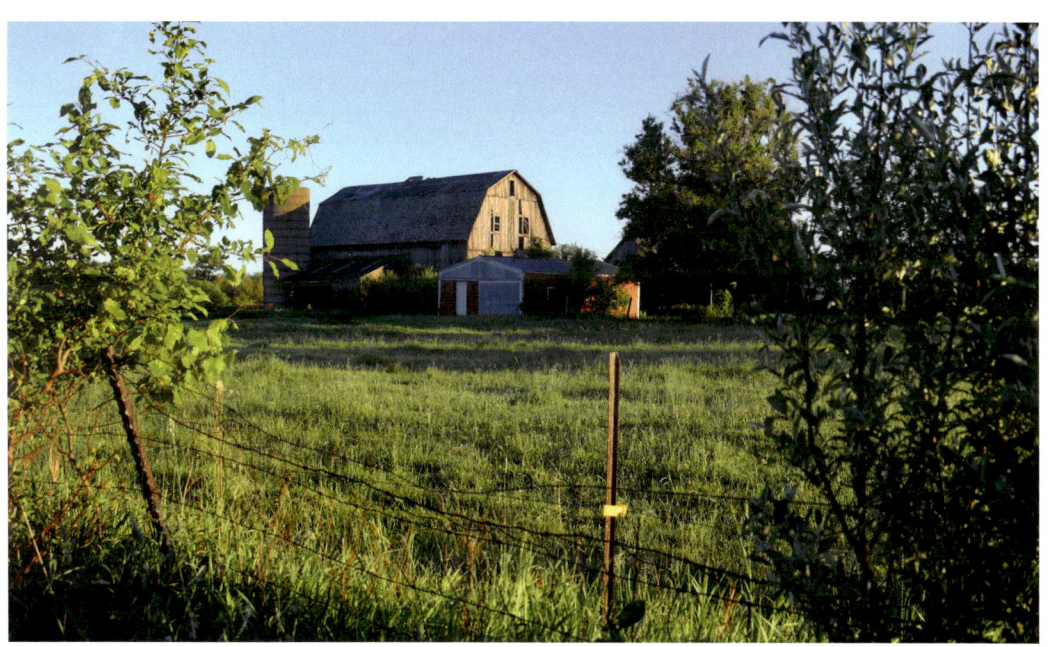

One of the many aging barns in the Thumb region, framed by a sagging wire fence.

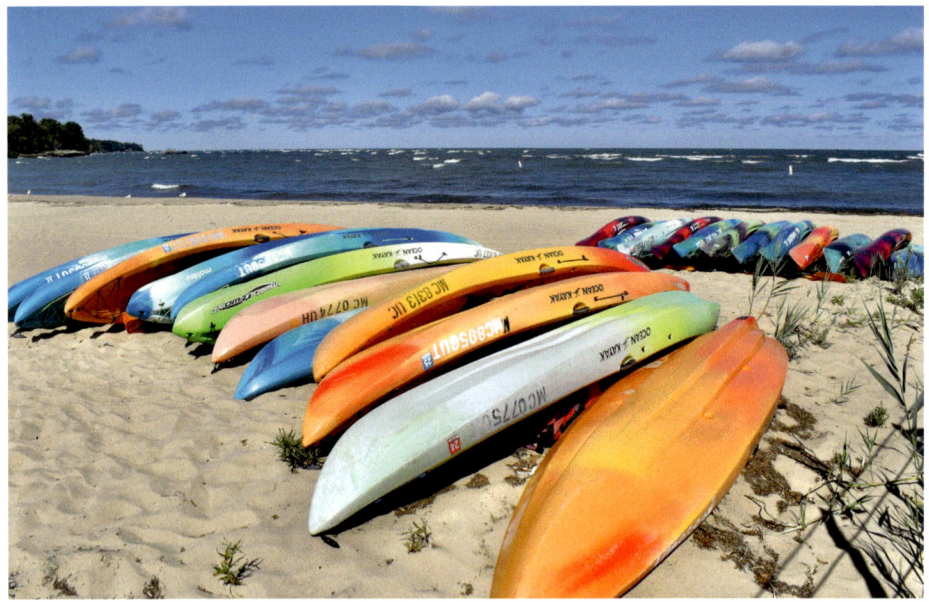

A picturesque rainbow of kayaks lounging on the sandy shore, ready to take a person on an adventure in Port Austin.

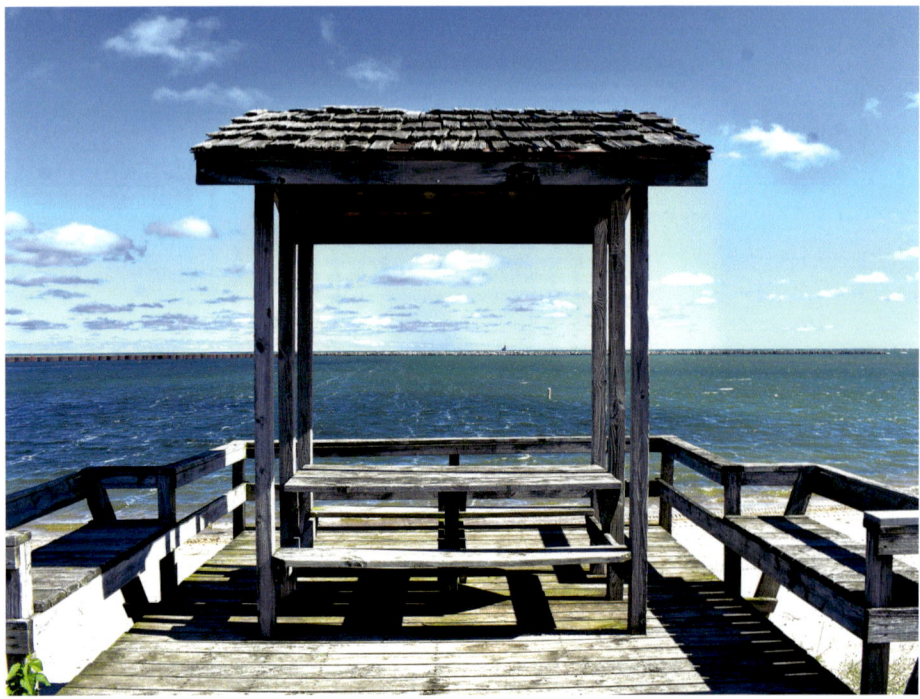

Benches beckon to the tired walker, to come and enjoy the sapphire waters of Lake Huron on a burning summer day.

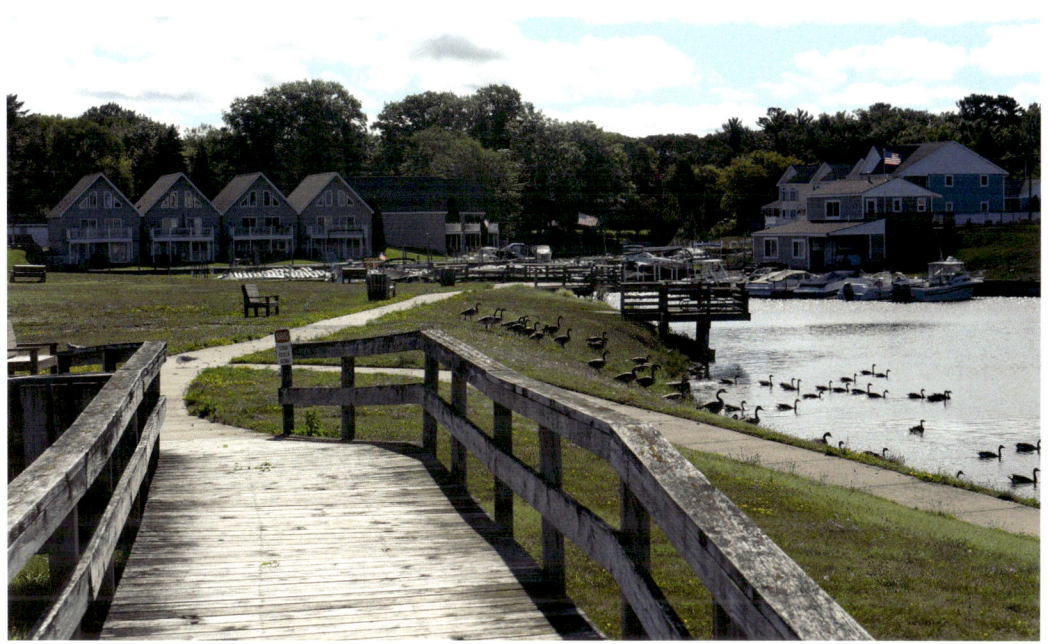

Bird Creek Park, a quaint stop in Port Austin, with its feathered friends.

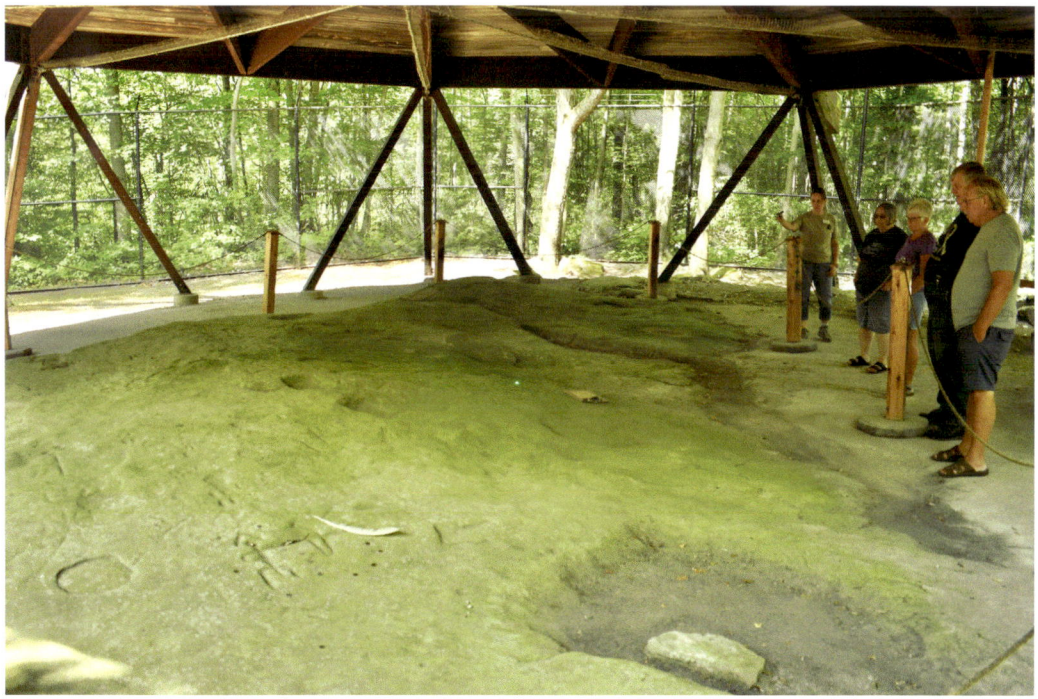

People listening intently to the guide while viewing the etchings at the Sanilac Petroglyphs Historic State Park.

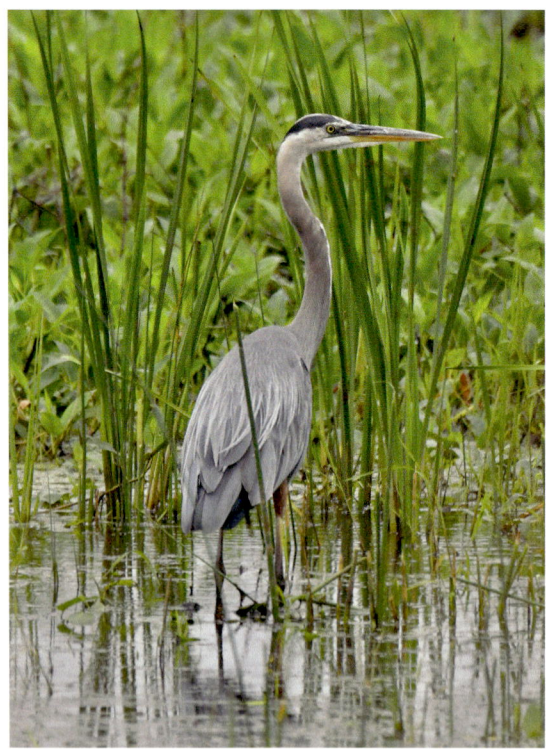

Left: A stately blue heron stands watch in one of the many wetlands found in the Thumb region.

Below: Shaggy ponies south of Marlette in a frigid 5 degrees.

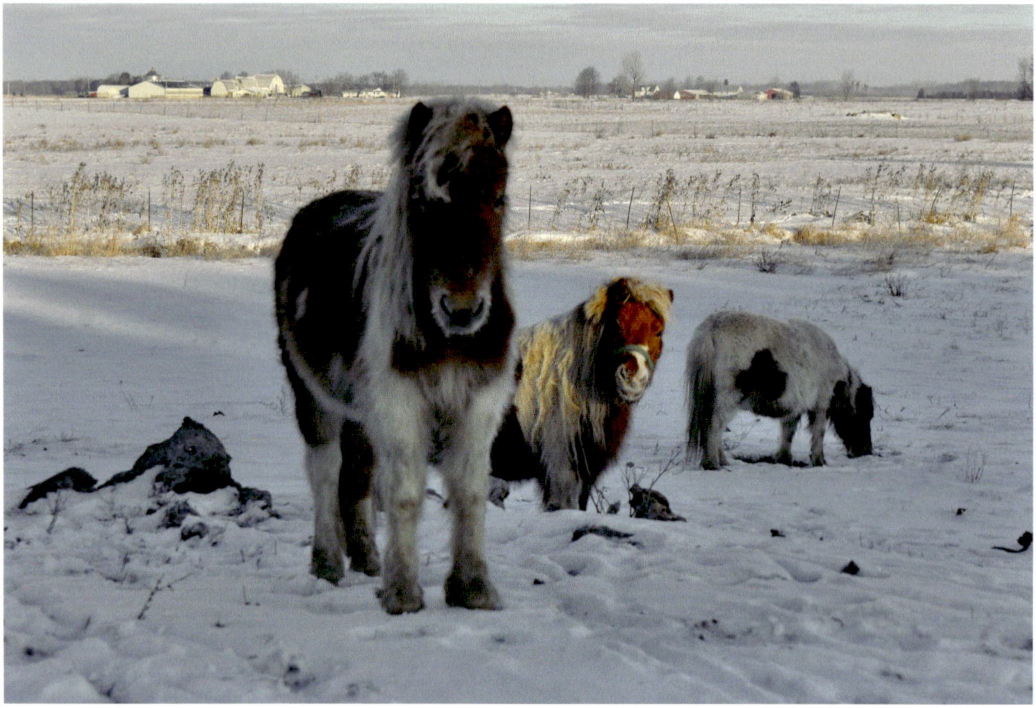

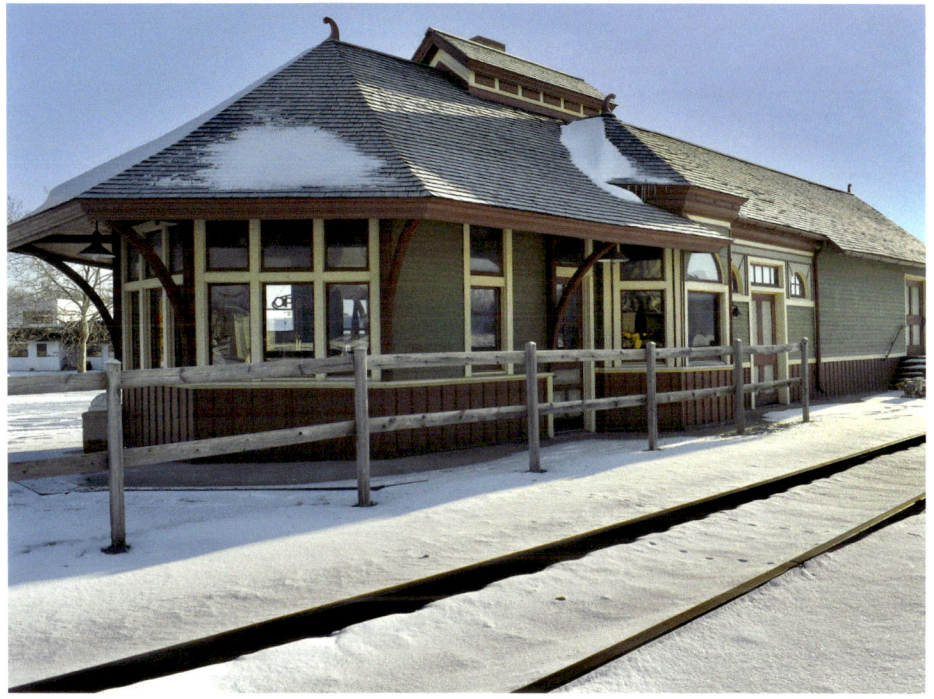

The 1890 Flint and Pere Marquette Railroad Depot, now a historical museum in Marlette.

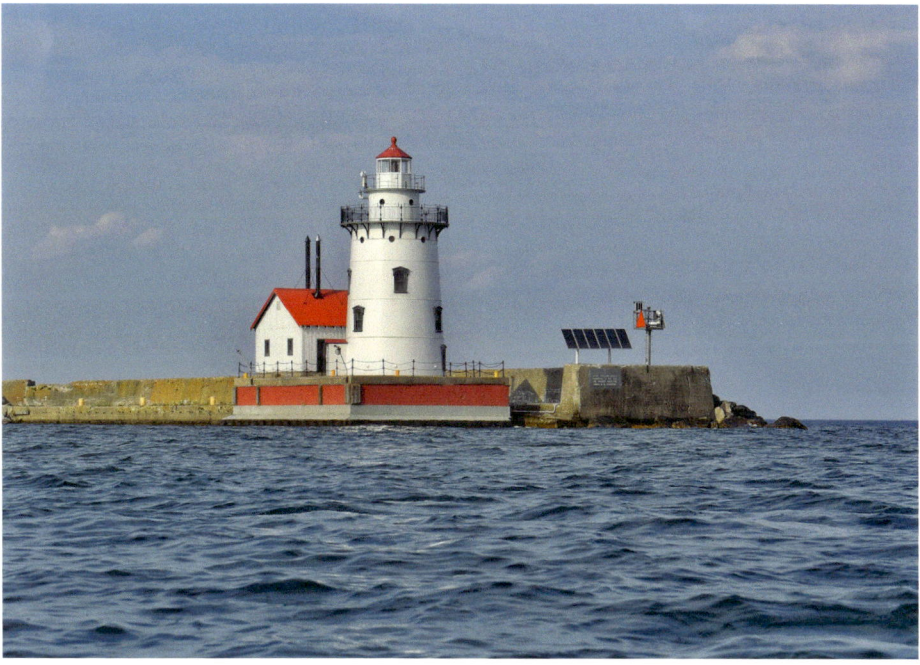

The Harbor Beach Lighthouse perched on the rocks jutting out from Lake Huron.

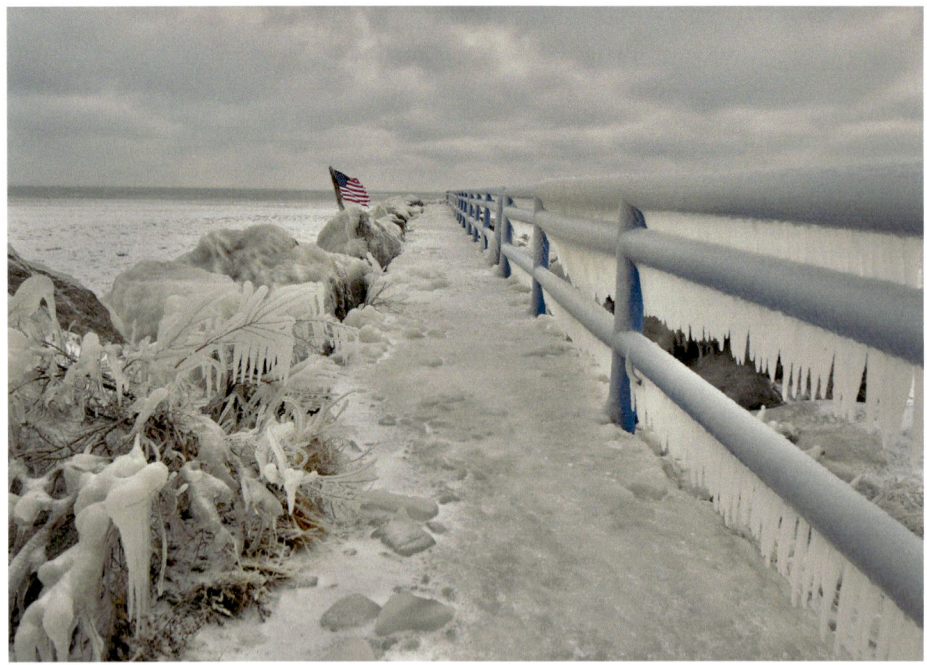

The ice encased pier at Lexington Harbor, a lone flag waving against the biting wind and the restless Lake Huron.

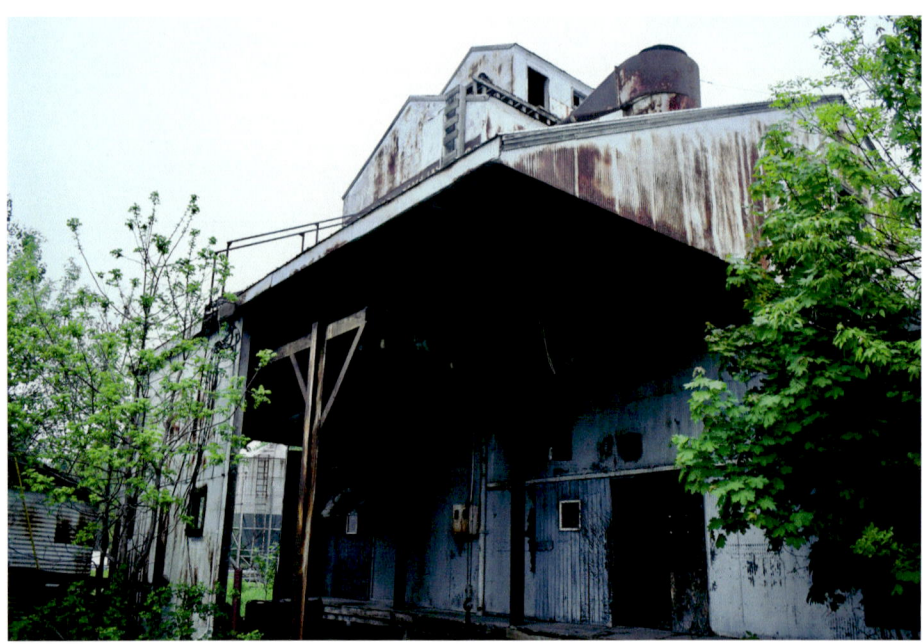

The Croswell Milling Company, slick with a cool rain, a remanent of the farming life of the past.

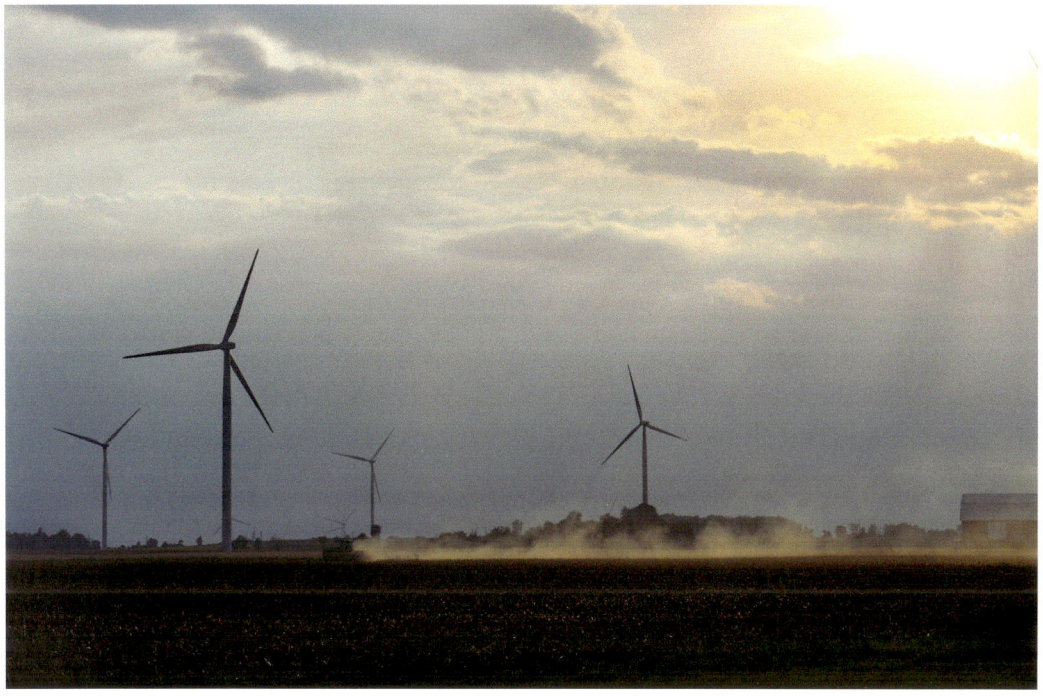

Hazy sunbeams illuminate ghostly wind turbines lording over a farmer plowing his dusty field.

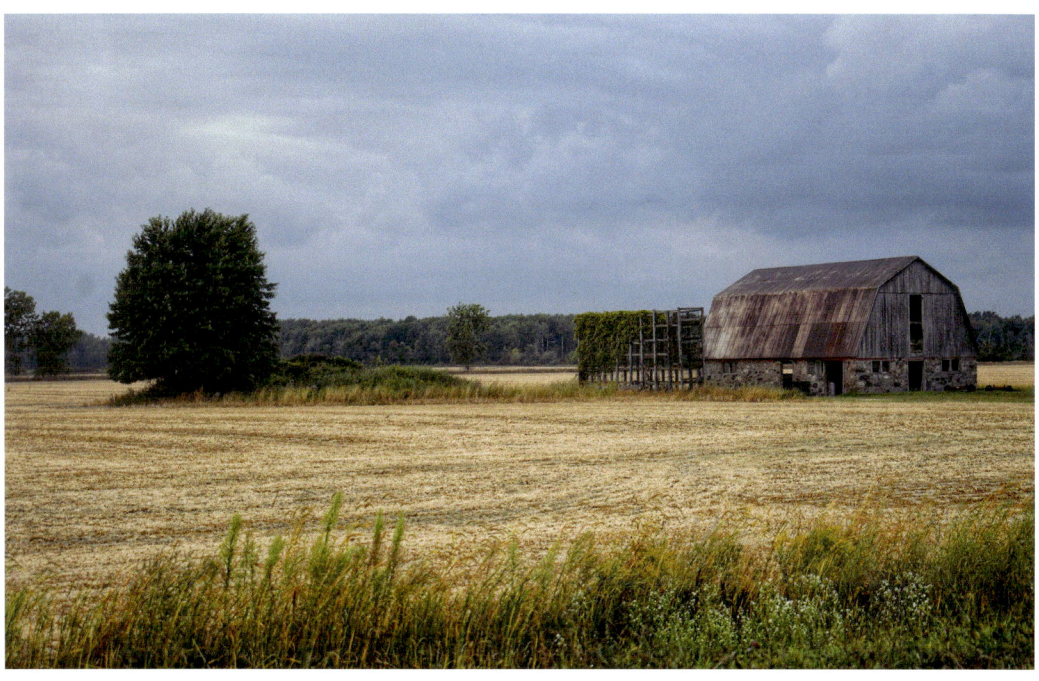

An ancient barn still standing against the elements.

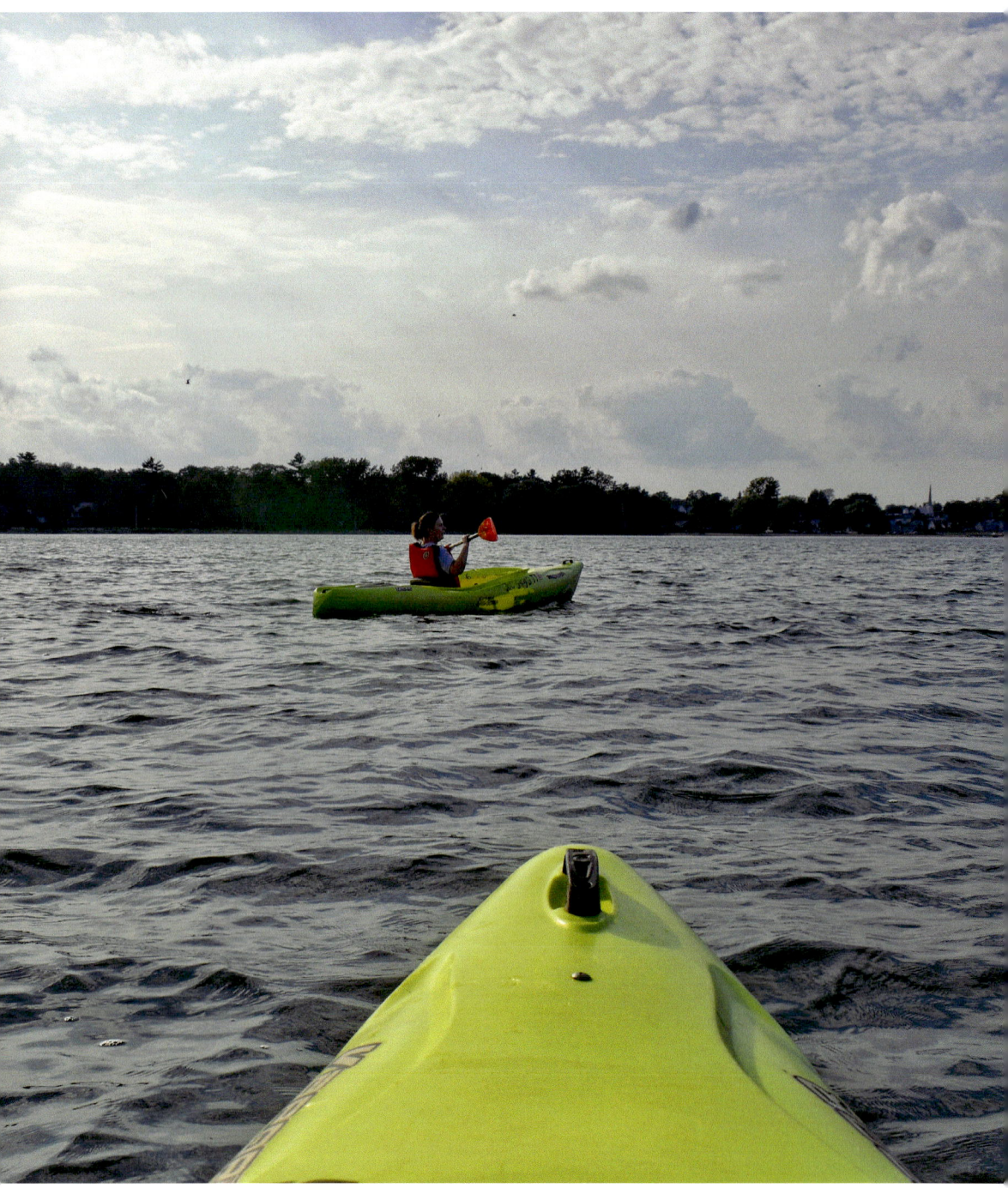

A kayaker's view of Harbor Beach's harbor with a fellow paddler looking for the shipwrecks sunken there.

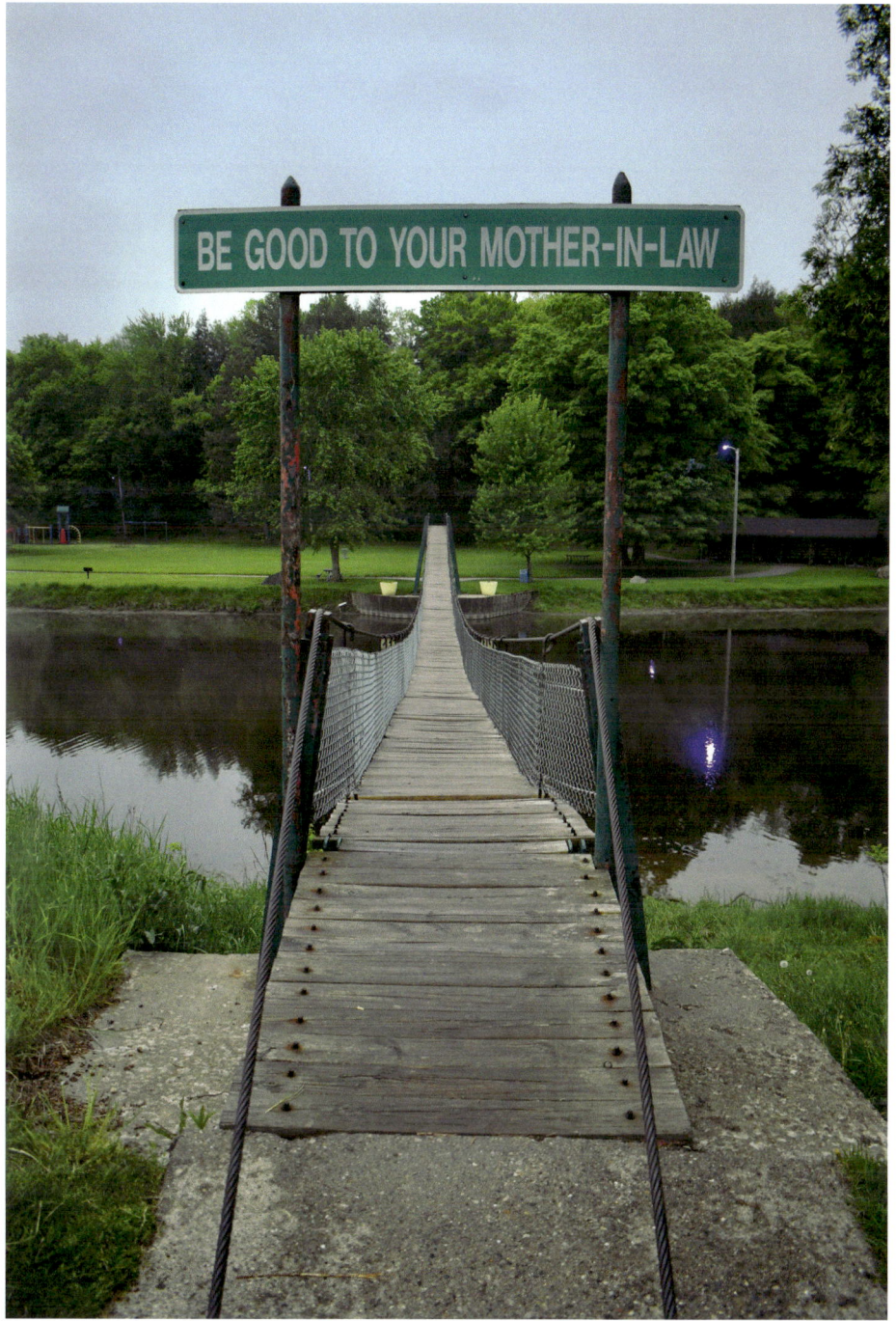

The Croswell Swinging Bridge leaving visitors with a playful message.

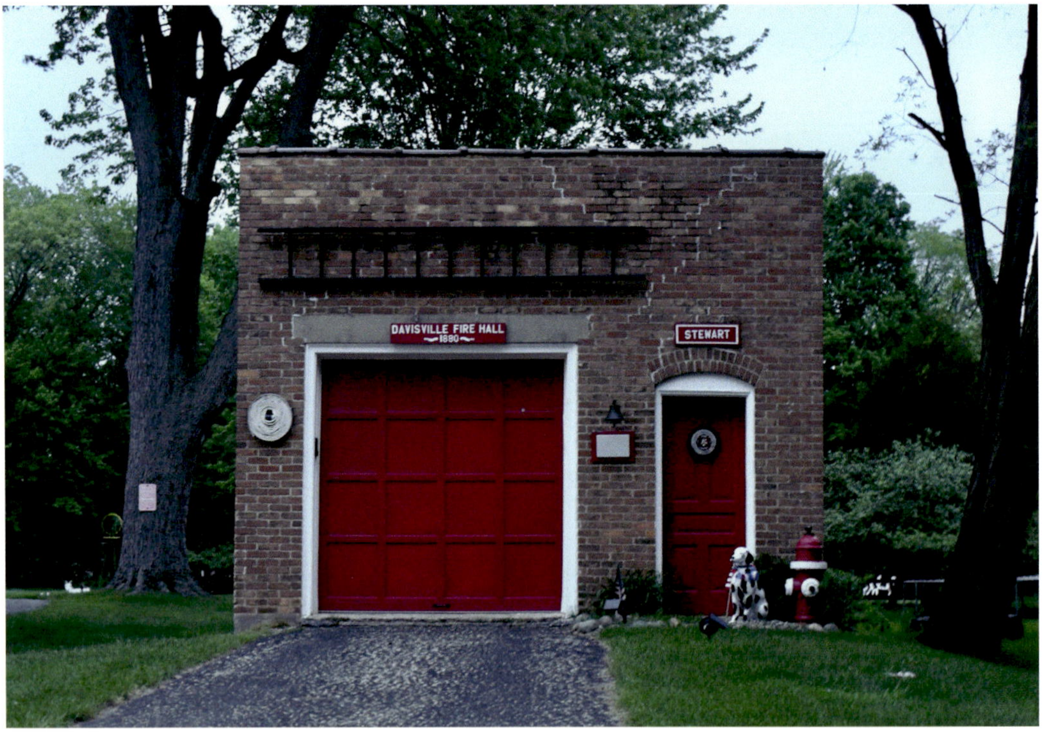

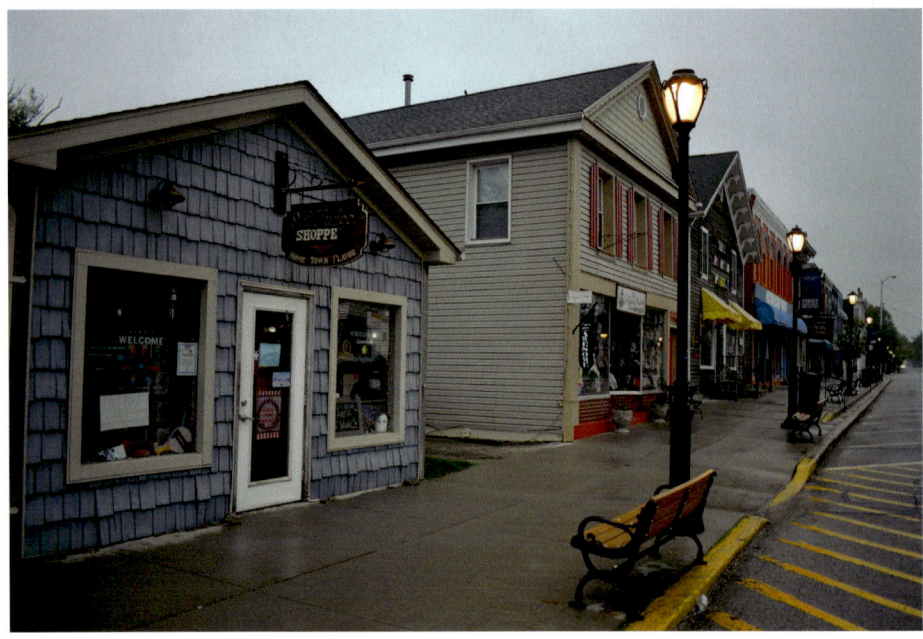

The tiny, cheerful Davisville Fire Hall with its complimentary dalmatian still preserved in Croswell.

Lexington's main street at dusk lined with eclectic shops to peruse at leisure.

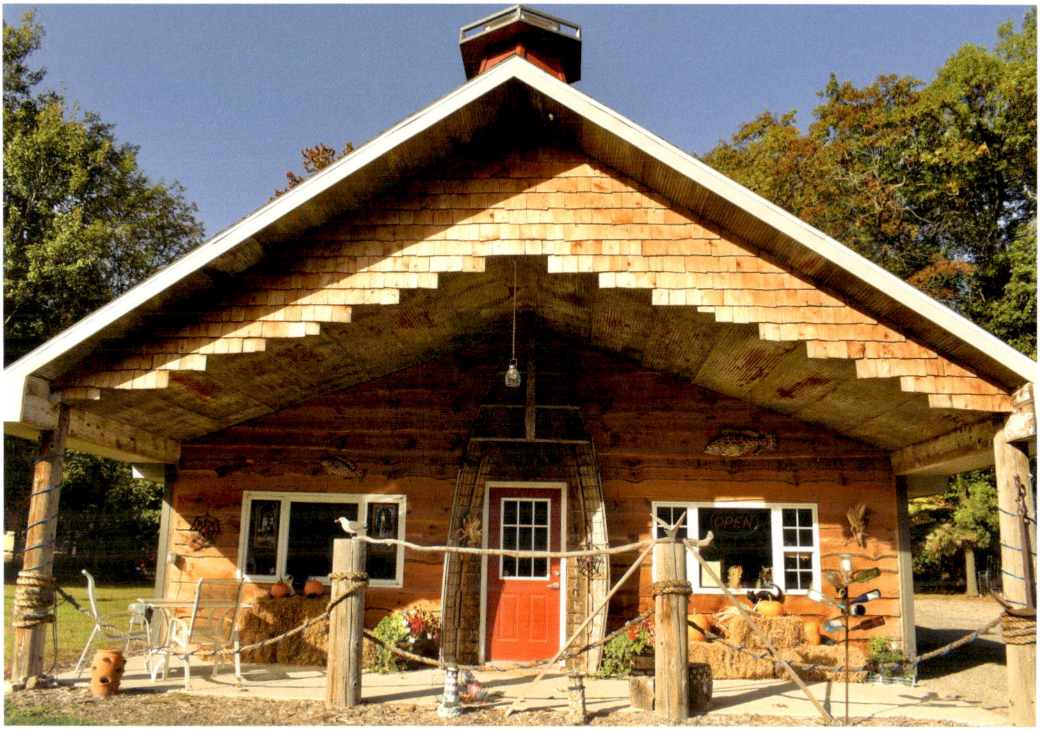

Shipwreck Distillery dotted with pumpkins in the fall.

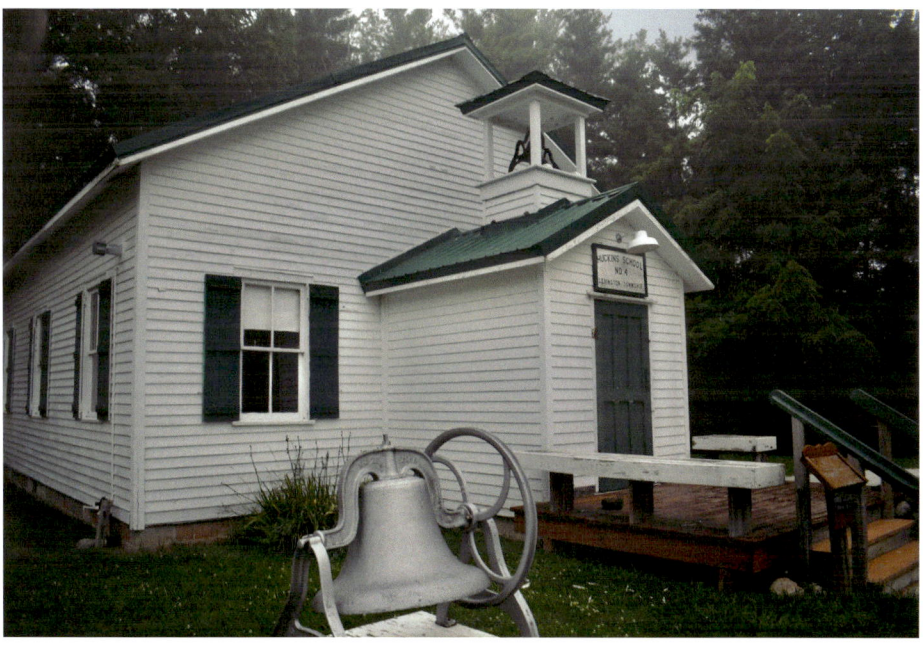

The functioning centennial schoolhouse at the Sanilac County Historic Village and Museum.

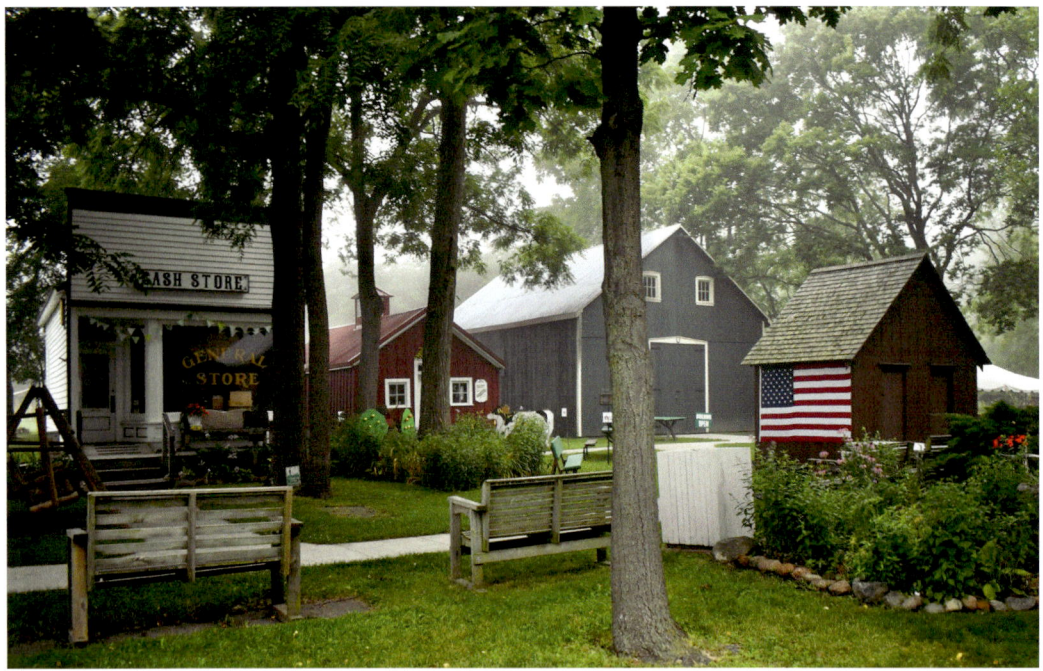

The Sanilac County Village, with its general store and dairy museum cloaked in fog.

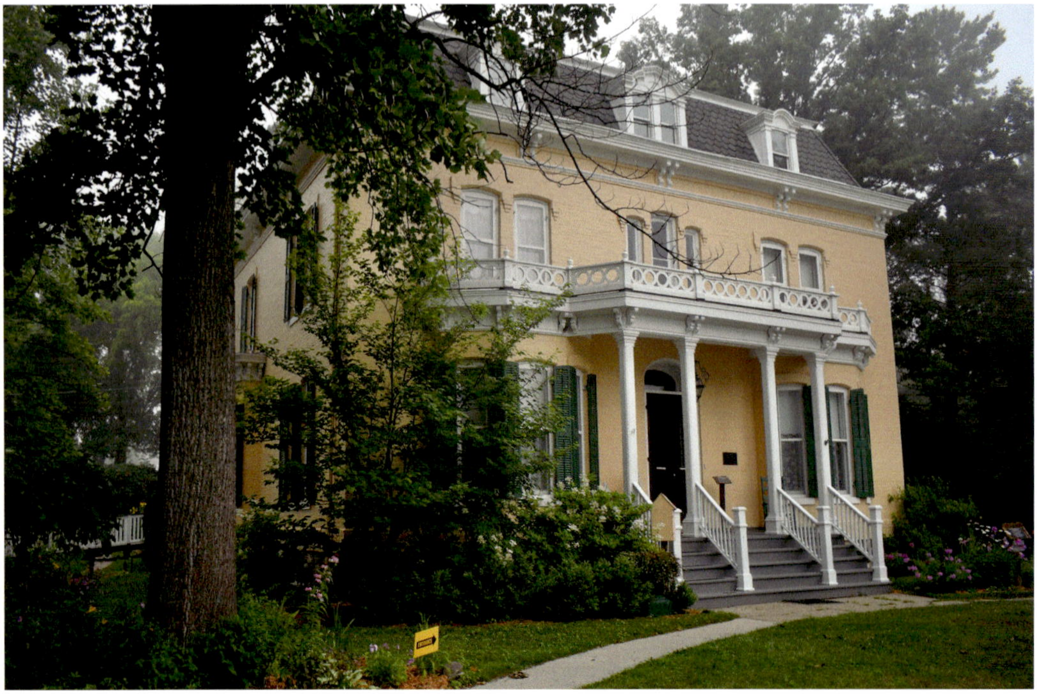

A beautifully restored mansion with white trim housing the Sanilac County Historic Museum.

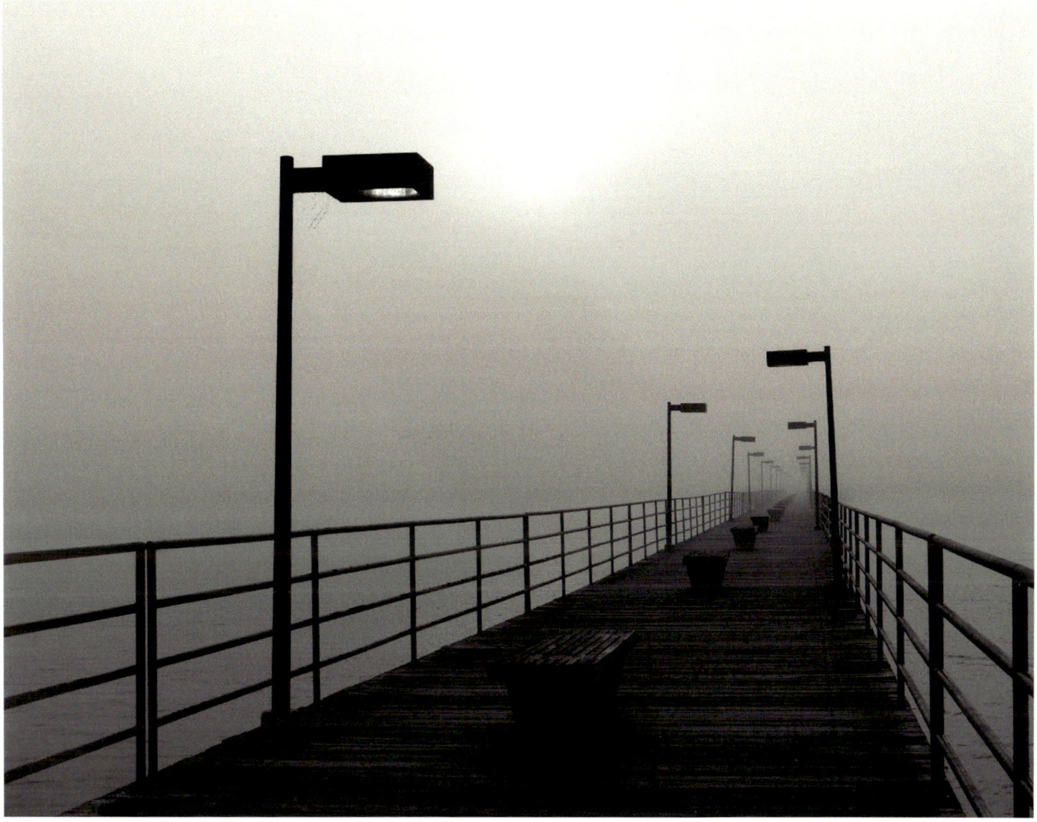

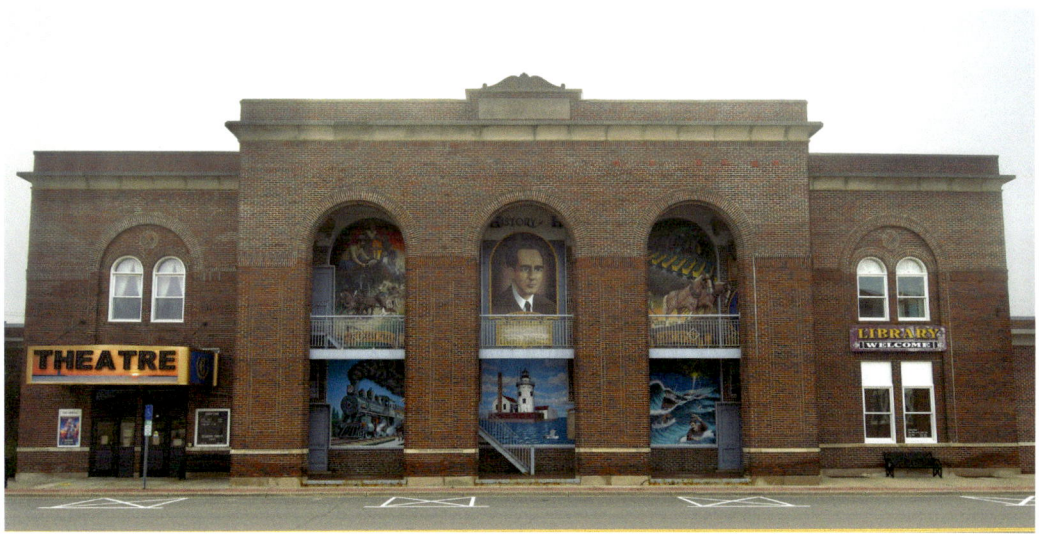

Fog swirls around a pier leading into the bowels of Lake Huron.

Painted murals depicting historical events adorn the Harbor Beach Theater.

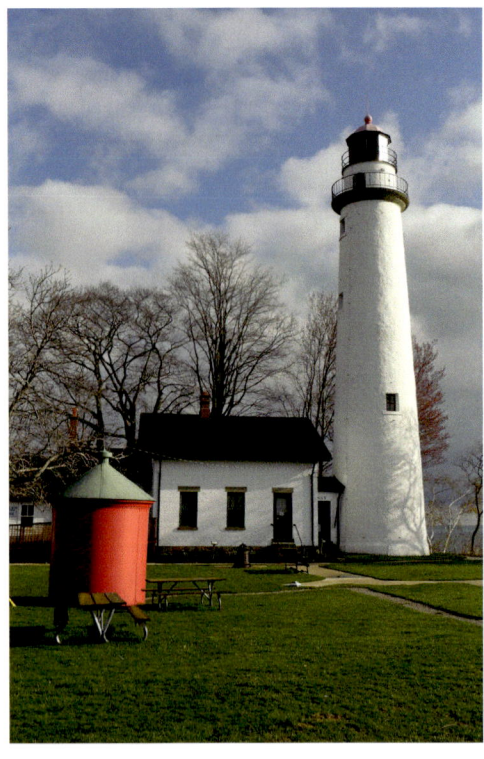

Left: Pointe Aux Barques Lighthouse standing guard over Lake Huron since 1847 in Huron County.

Below: Solitude beckons at a beach riddled with glacial stones on Lake Huron.

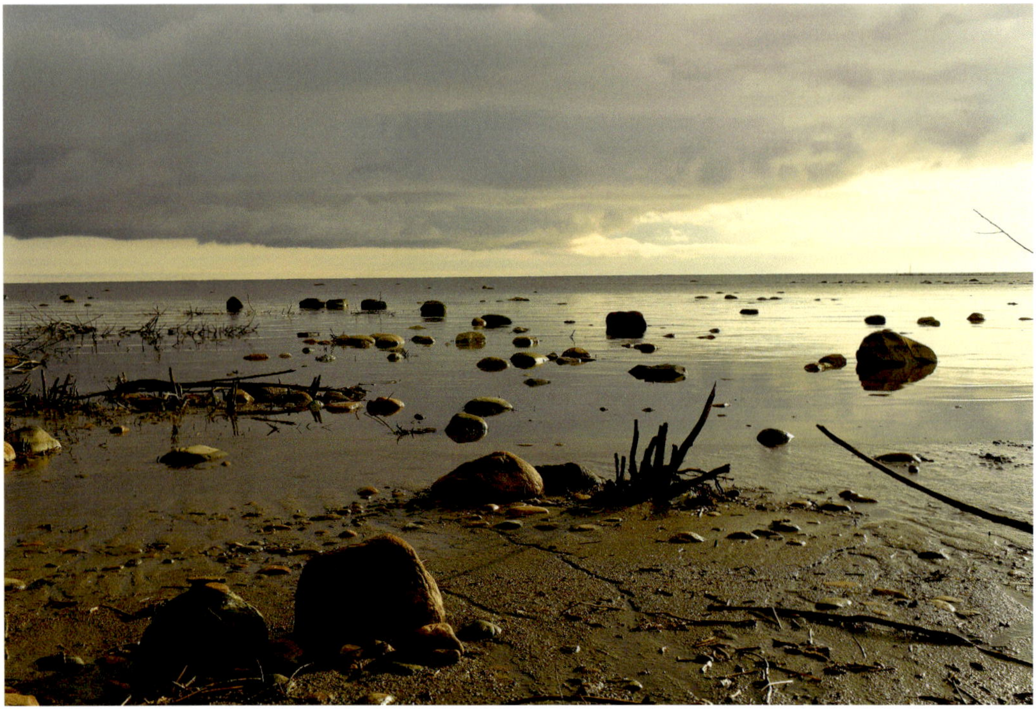

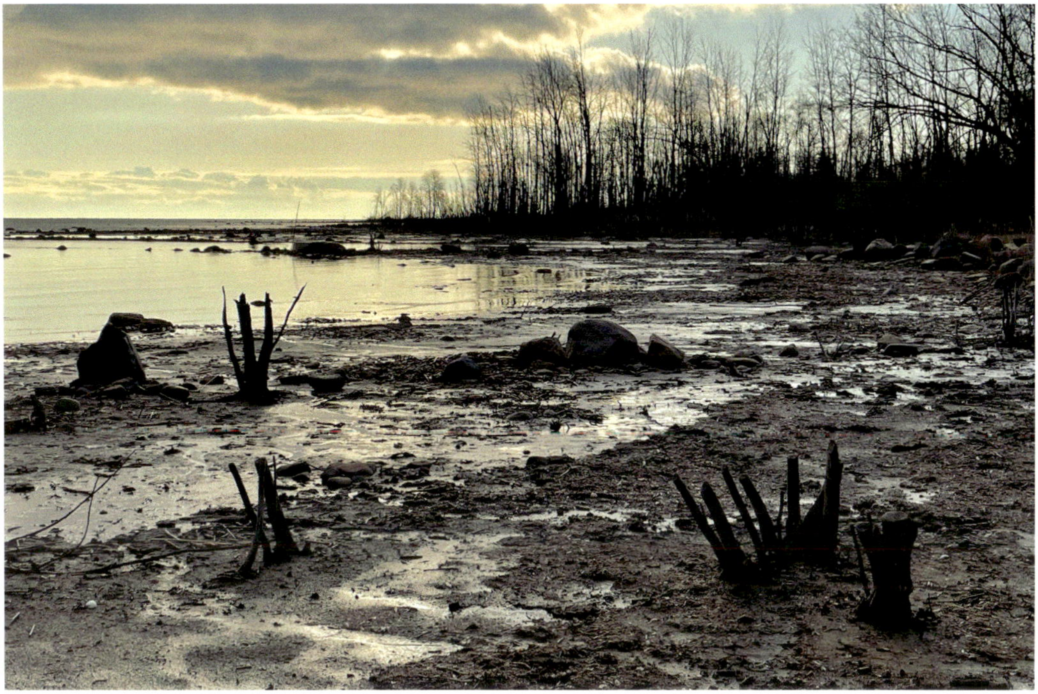

Harsh spring rays paint a moody image at the Kernan Memorial Nature Sanctuary.

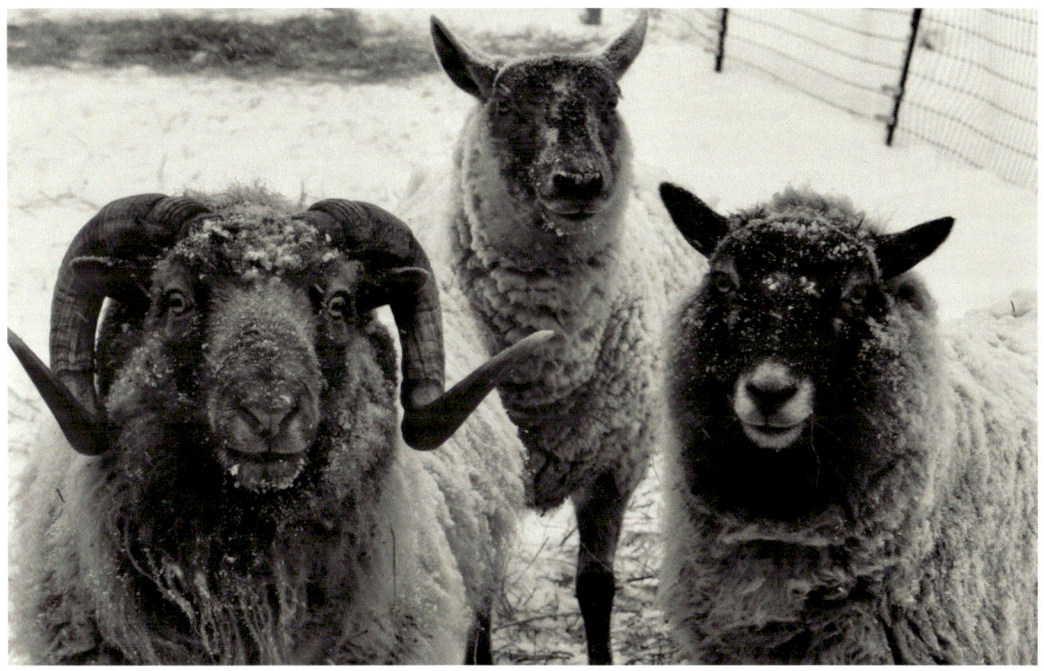

A ram with his two lady ewes waiting for the arrival of spring.

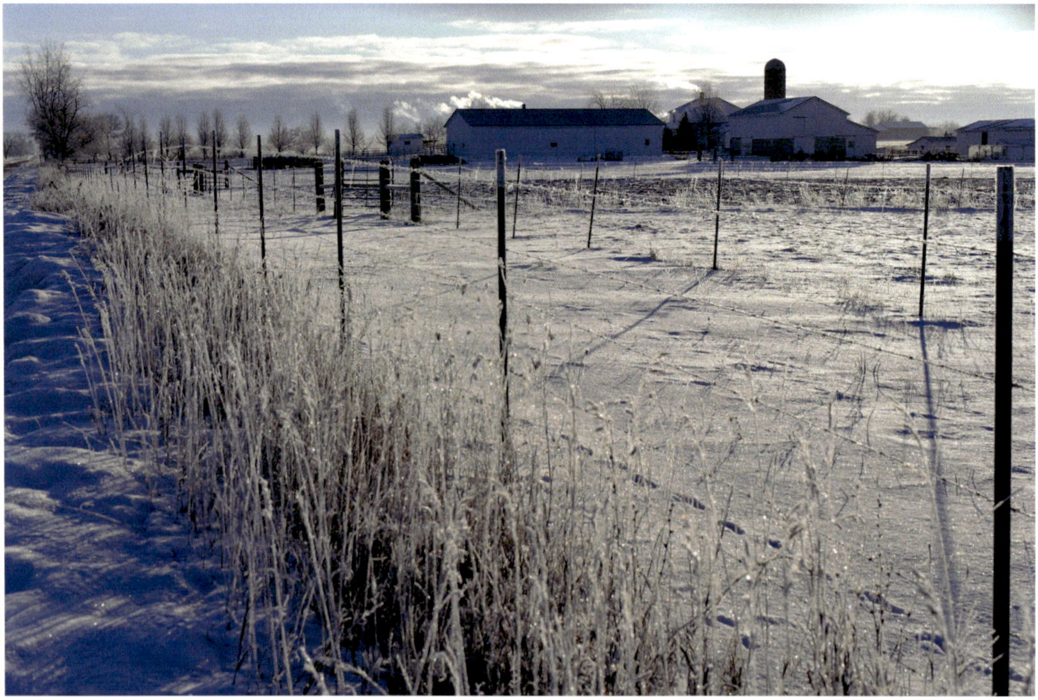

A frosty, frozen day in Sanilac County.

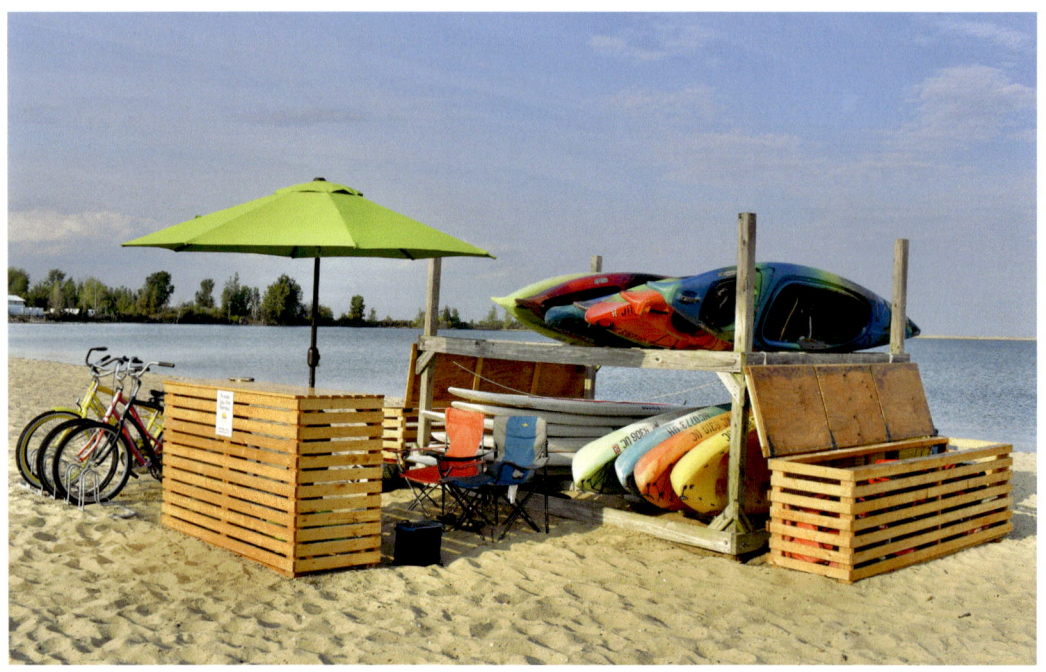

Kayaks popping with vibrant colors await a jaunt on the watery Harbor Beach Harbor.

2

Southeast Region

Home to the Blue Water Bridge, Port Huron banks the rollicking St. Clair River and the vast, cerulean Lake Huron to the north. The city embraces belonging to the Blue Water area and a scenic riverwalk arcs along the river from the Blue Water Bridge down to a small wetland area with secretive mudpuppies and playful minks. A statue of a young Thomas Edison stands below the bridge and signifies when the inventor's family moved to the city in 1854. Along Main Street rest many notable buildings, their beautiful facades remnants of years past. Prior to the Civil War, the city was an important terminal for the Underground Railroad due to its proximity to Canada. During the Civil War, many people from around the world immigrated to the United States through Port Huron, second only to New York City. Another notable piece of history is the city built the first global underwater railroad tunnel in 1890. After visiting the waterfront, there are many other attractions to enjoy including a vintage lighthouse with historic buildings, an eclectic coffeehouse, and a delightful downtown for shopping.

While spending time in Port Huron, head to the Fort Gratiot Lighthouse, Michigan's oldest lighthouse, at 2802 Omar Street, Port Huron. A metal, spiral staircase leads to a catwalk where there are breathtaking views of Lake Huron, the St. Clair River, Point Edward, Ontario, and the Blue Water Bridge. Built in 1814 during the War of 1812, the lighthouse guarded the juncture of Lake Huron and the St. Clair River. The lighthouse is part of the Fort Gratiot Light Station and is surrounded by other historical dwellings, including a military hospital with a bedded patient and concerned doctor display. A gift shop with Michigan items stands near the entrance to the property.

Another compelling spot along the riverwalk is the Huron Lightship at 800 Prospect Place, Port Huron. A lightship is a floating lighthouse used in watery regions where it was too pricey to construct a lighthouse. The Huron was the last operating lightship on the Great Lakes and was retired in 1970 after fifty years of service. With its large, bold, white lettering against its sturdy black hull, the Huron houses numerous fascinating artifacts and an underwater camera with live feed of the bottom of the St. Clair River.

Take a walk through history at the Thomas Edison Depot Museum housed in the vintage Fort Gratiot train depot constructed in 1858 at 510 Edison Parkway, Port Huron. Standing in the shadow of the Blue Water Bridge, the depot is where Thomas Edison worked from 1859 to 1863 as a news reporter. The museum showcases the inventions and ingenuity of Edison and traces his life from Ohio to Port Huron, highlighting his great successes along with his frustrating setbacks. A classical baggage car on the tracks outside recreates the inventor's printing shop and chemistry lab.

At the entrance of Raven Café at 932 Military Street, Port Huron, perches a large, ebony raven statue which could have flown out of Edgar Allen Poe's poem, "The Raven." The coffeehouse caters to the beloved author and artifacts related to him adorn its interior. Books line the walls upstairs and groups of sofas for sitting create an intimate, cozy setting. Feast on foods such as the "House of Usher" Turkey Deluxe or the "Pit & Pendulum" grilled Reuben while sipping on a Deadman's Reach brewed coffee. On certain evenings, enjoy live music or a trivia night with friends.

Emmett is a tiny village that can be missed with the blink of an eye. A small, former antique shop with a large Duff Beer sculpture and ornate outhouse, once used for outdoor theatrics, sit on the main street along with a little hardware store that boasts it has everything. Nearby is a notable tree farm and an apple orchard.

Centennial Pines Tree Farm at 2775 Bricker Road, Wales Township, is a family-owned business that has been in existence since 1850 when it started with crop and cattle farming. Centennial spans six generations and encompasses 120 acres with over 30,000 trees. Walk through the snow dusted fields around the holidays to cut down the perfect Christmas tree while inhaling the heady scents of pine, fir, and spruce. The friendly workers will shake and wrap your tree, getting it ready for transport. The farm also offers hayrides on weekends, wreaths, roping, and grave blankets.

For fall fun, head to Rickert Apple Orchard at 11036 Metcalf Road, Brockway. Stroll through the warm fields with hunched, gnarled trees ladened with succulent apples and pick your own fruit. Then head to the store packed with a large variety of delicious apples, such as Honey Crisp, Crimson Red, Roma, and Gala, some of which are vintage varieties and are not available at grocery stores. The store also sells seasonal vegetables, their own pressed cider, golden honey pulled from the hives, and soft, sweet, handmade donuts. On occasion, the family will do some baking and offer homemade pies and apple bars.

Yale, whose roots extend back to 1889, is a city that is full of bologna. Known unofficially as the Bologna Capital of the World, the town hosts the Yale Bologna Festival every year since 1989, where fried bologna sandwiches or a link of bologna on a bun slathered in mustard are favorites. Historic buildings line its main street, including the Yale Hotel with its vintage facade, built in 1889.

Perched on the edge of Main Street is the quaint Red Dog Café at 208 South Main Street, Yale. Serving home-cooked favorites, all menu items have dog breeds in their name, such as toy poodle tuna melt or terrier turkey and bacon. The café is only open in the morning until 2:00 p.m. and is a great place to sit down with the locals and chat about farming and the weather.

At the end of town is a place dosed with nostalgia, an old A &W restaurant at 208 North Main Street, Yale. Pull up your car and order at an outside menu for curb side service that began in the 1920s. Savor all the favorites, from a frothy root beer float with their signature soda to a hefty double BBQ bacon crunch burger loaded with crispy, fried onions.

Port Huron State Game Area, with a gravel parking lot on M-136 between Wildcat Road and Cribbins Road, sprawls across Clyde and Grant Township. The forested area, through which the Black River snakes, is a restful place encompassing over 6,000 acres. The site has over 5 miles of trails and is a great place to pull off and stretch your legs. Meander through the woods of oak and maple while listening to the bubbling song of the river. Hunting is prohibited between May 15 and September 10, so the spot is great for a little solitary reflection. You may spot ospreys dipping their talons into the water for fish or wild turkeys strutting through the trees.

Avoca is a small town that used to be a stop on the Port Huron and Northwestern Railway. An old grain elevator, with rust decaying its sides and which rattles in the wind, is the last remanent of that era. The CSX tracks are gone, and their path has been converted into the Wadhams to Avoca Trail, the trailhead which starts in the town and where there is a gravel lot for parking. This non-motorized path of 12 miles is the perfect place for a hike. The centerpiece on the trail is an antiquated railway trellis from the 1800s spanning the snaking Mill Creek below. Horseback riders are frequently spotted on the trail at the north end.

For an experience like no other, wander the heavenly scented lavender fields of the Indigo Lavender Farm at 631 North Van Dyke Road, Imlay City. The farm's flowers are in full bloom under the shining July sun with rows and rows of purple blossoms, ready to cut and take home. On the edge of the fields are patches of sunflowers, providing a golden-dotted backdrop for pictures. The charming gift store has everything lavender, from creamy fragrant soap to plants. In August, the farm hosts Indigo Fest with live music, food trucks, and Michigan vendors.

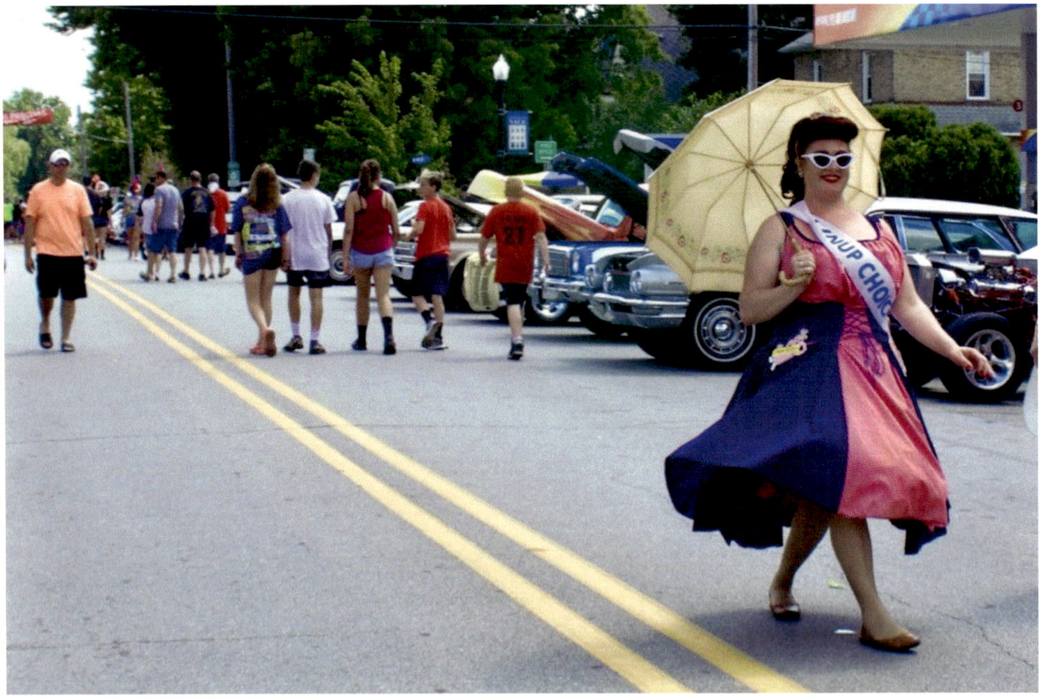

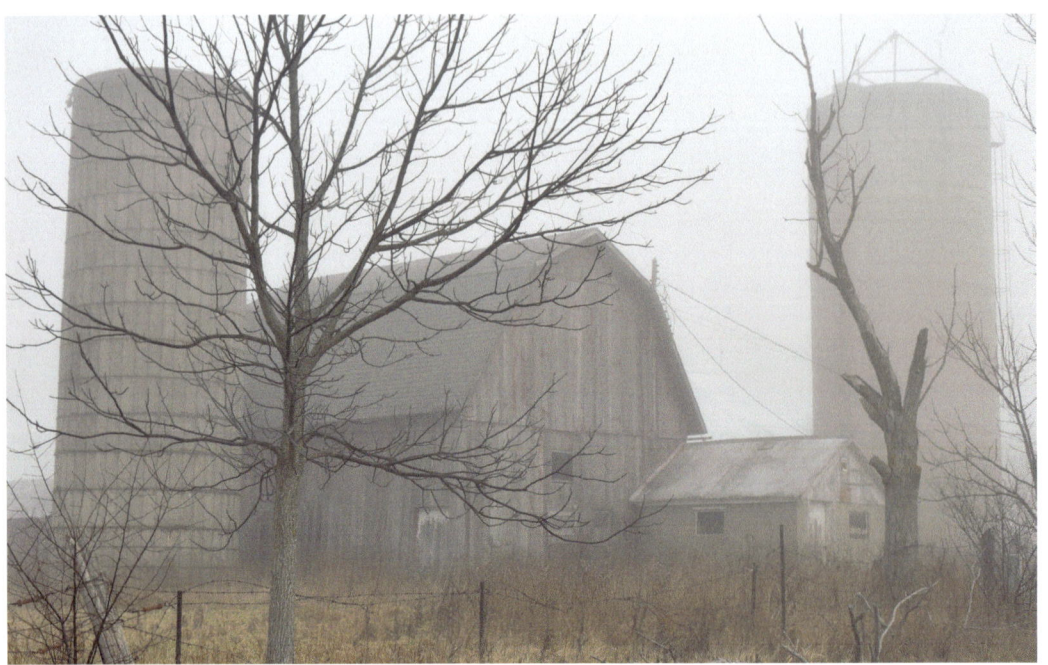

Yale Bologna Festival with vintage cars parked along Main Street.

A barn with its hand-cut planks, shrouded in the morning mist.

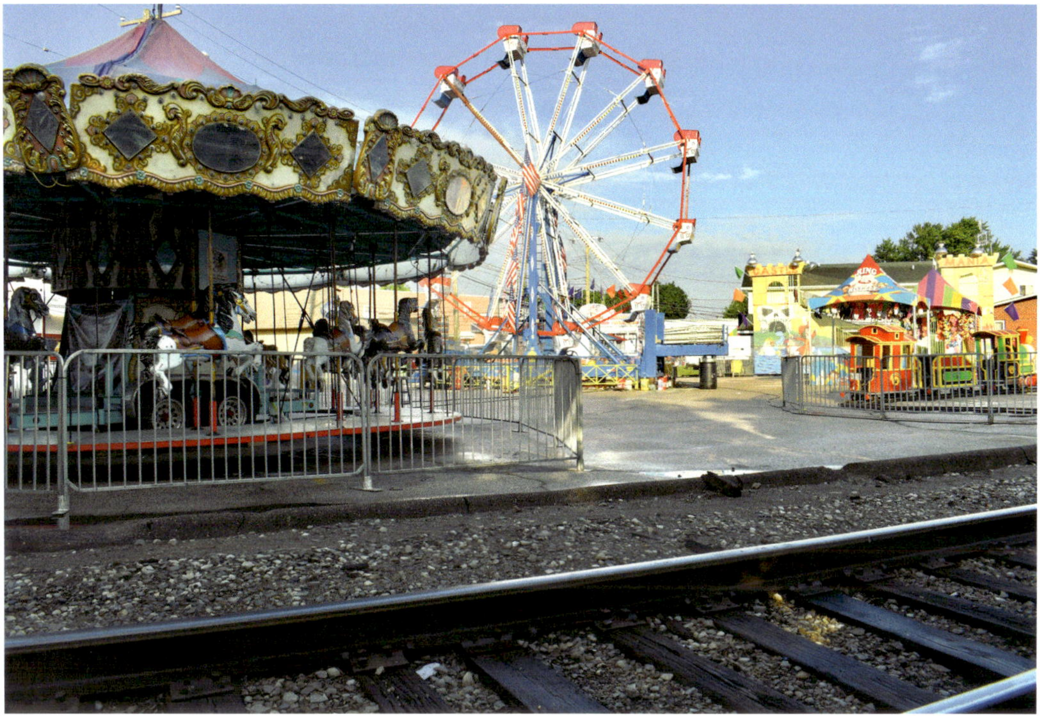

Above: The Brown City carnival perched next to the railroad tracks.

Right: Nighttime in Capac, the snow dyed gold by the hazy streetlamps.

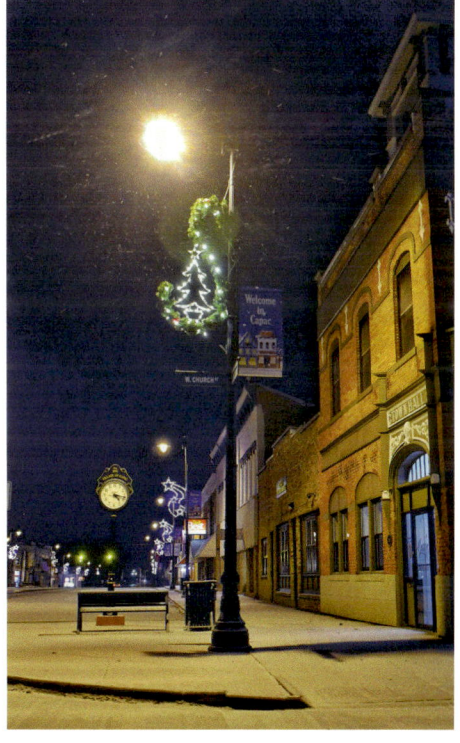

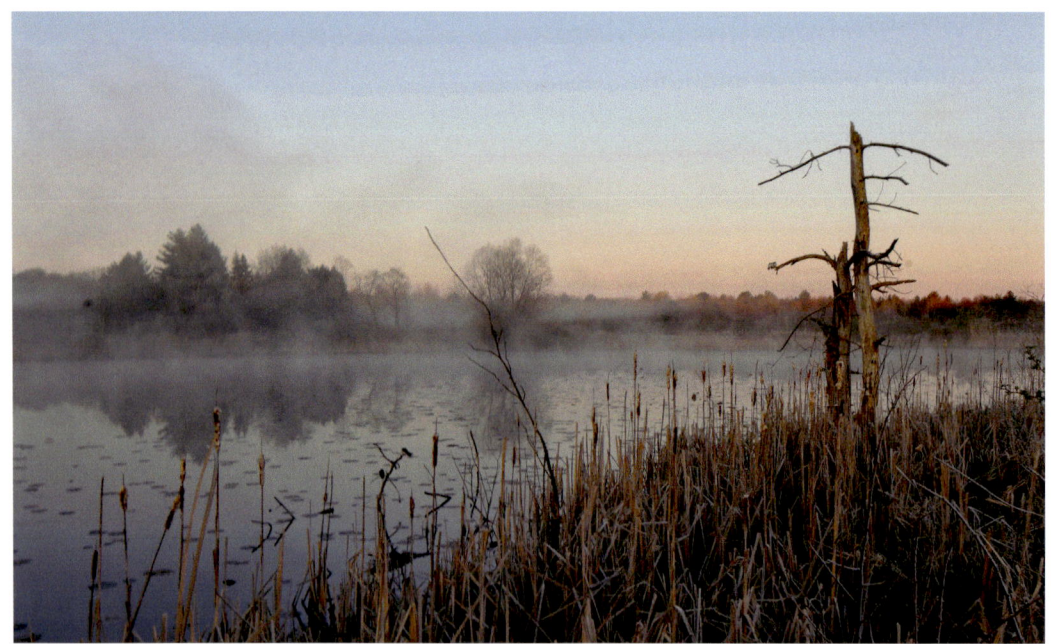

The fog drifts over a silent wetland, greeted by a pastel morning in Clyde Township.

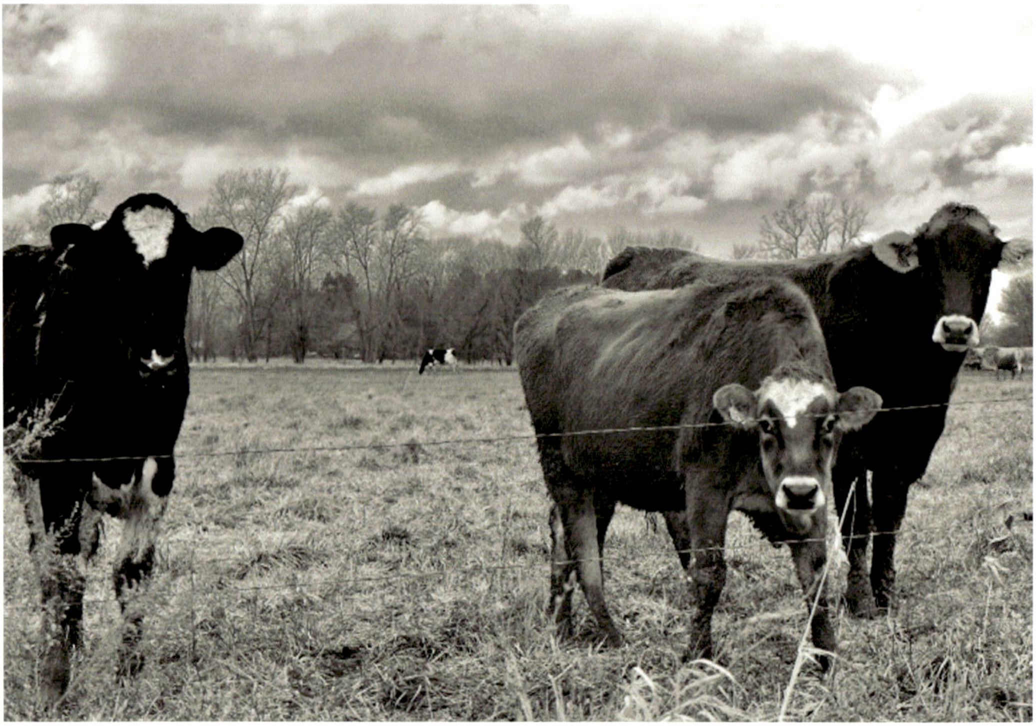

Mean-mugging dairy cows.

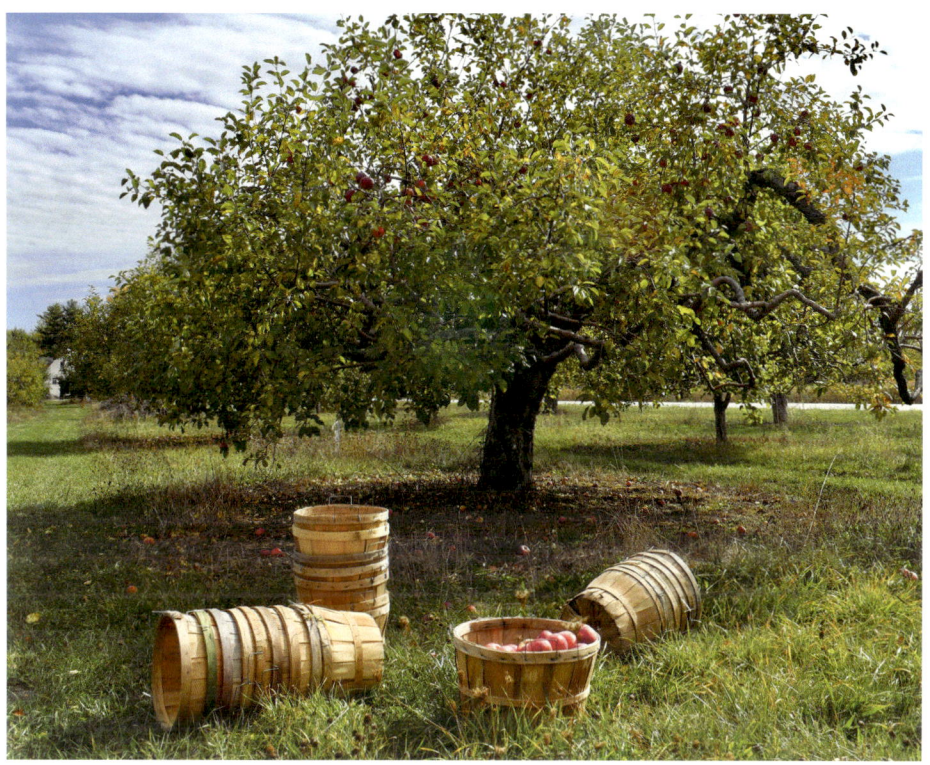

Juicy, crimson apples fill wicker baskets on a radiant sunny autumn day at Rickert Orchard.

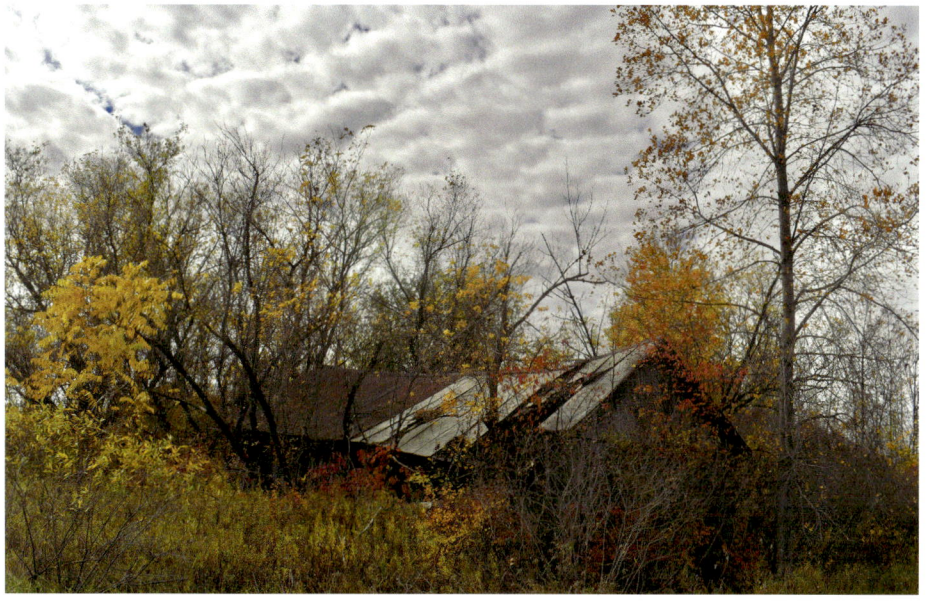

Nature consuming an old, wooden shed under a sullen sky.

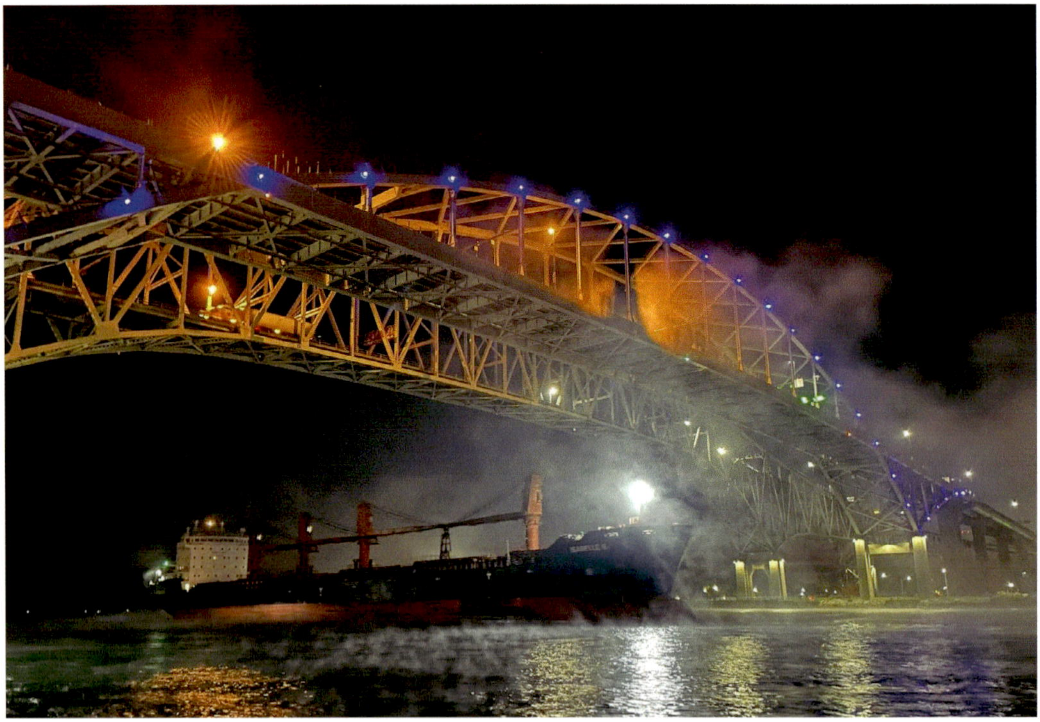

The Blue Water Bridge under which a freighter passes, its lights piercing the heavy fog.

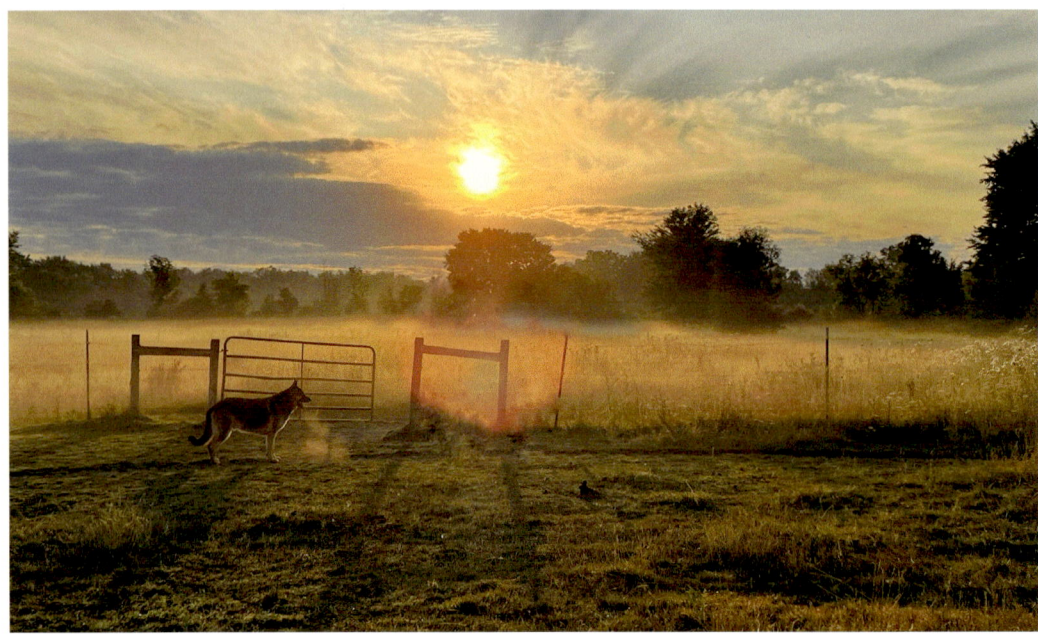

A farm dog pants clouds of steam on an early chilly morning.

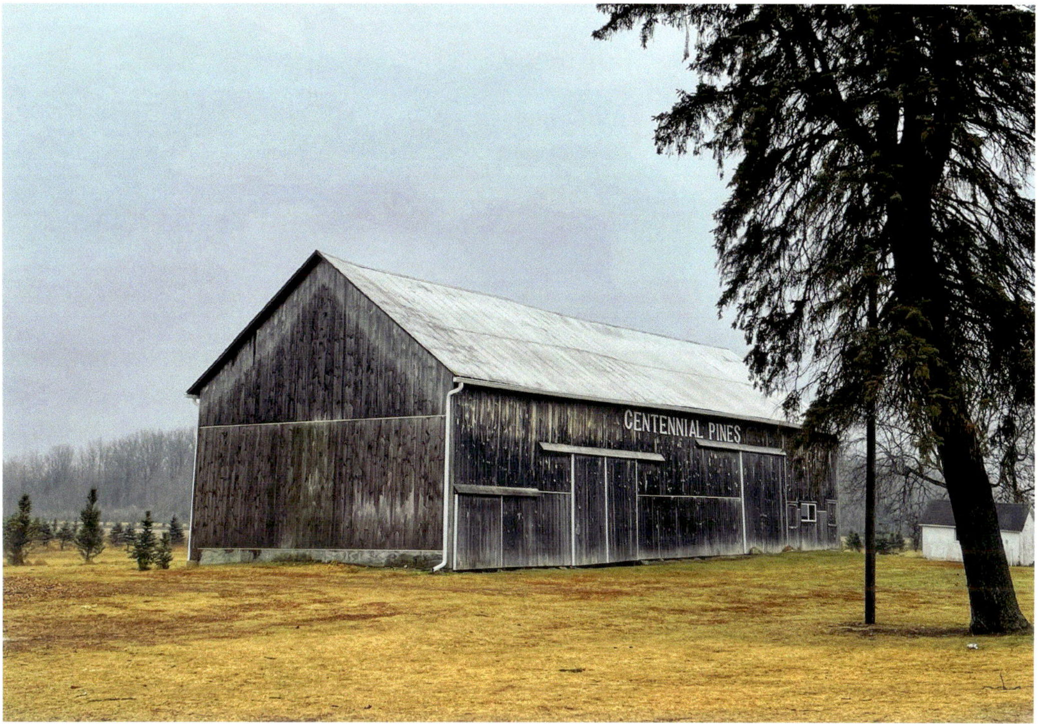

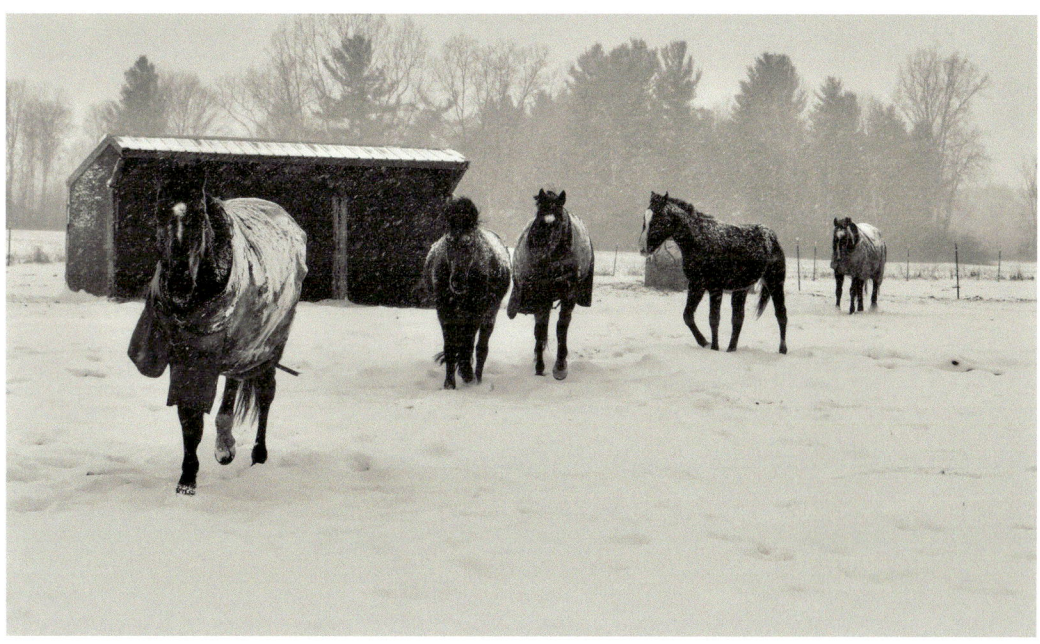

Centennial Pines, where families go to harvest fragrant Christmas trees.

Horses walking through the floating snowflakes of a winter storm.

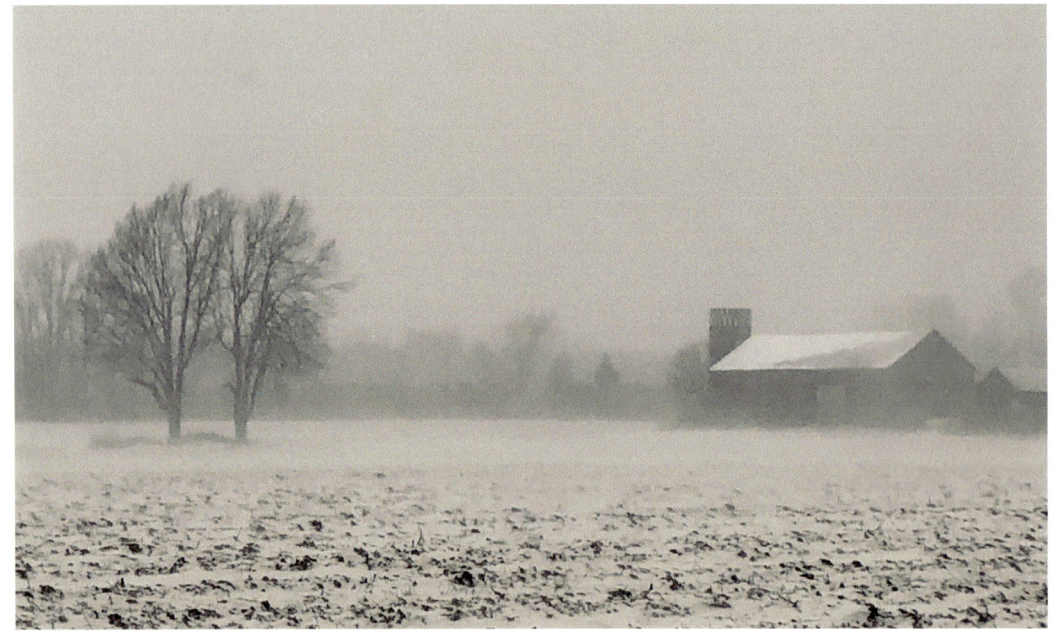

Fierce biting winds swirl around a stoic barn.

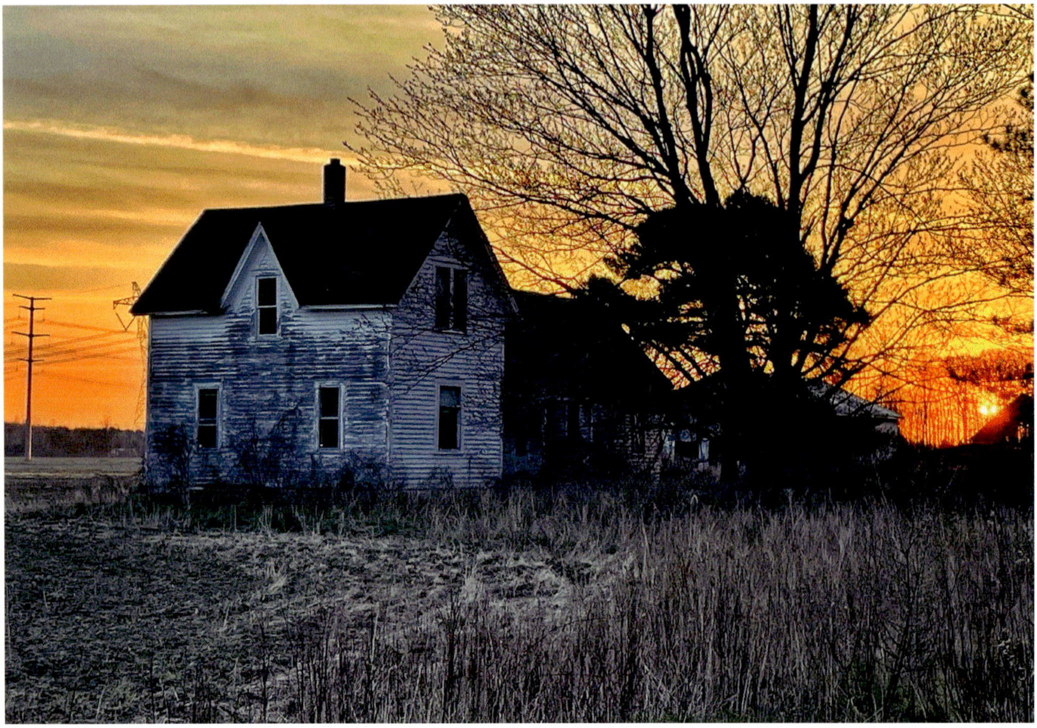

An old farmhouse welcomes the glowing dawn.

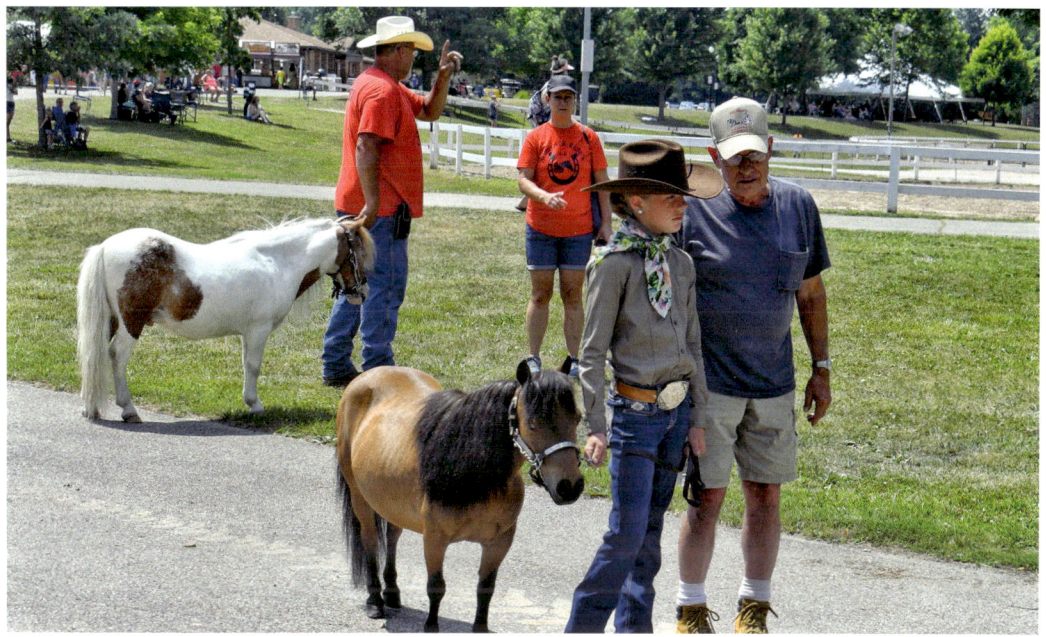

Last minute advice before heading into the show ring at the Goodells 4-H Fair.

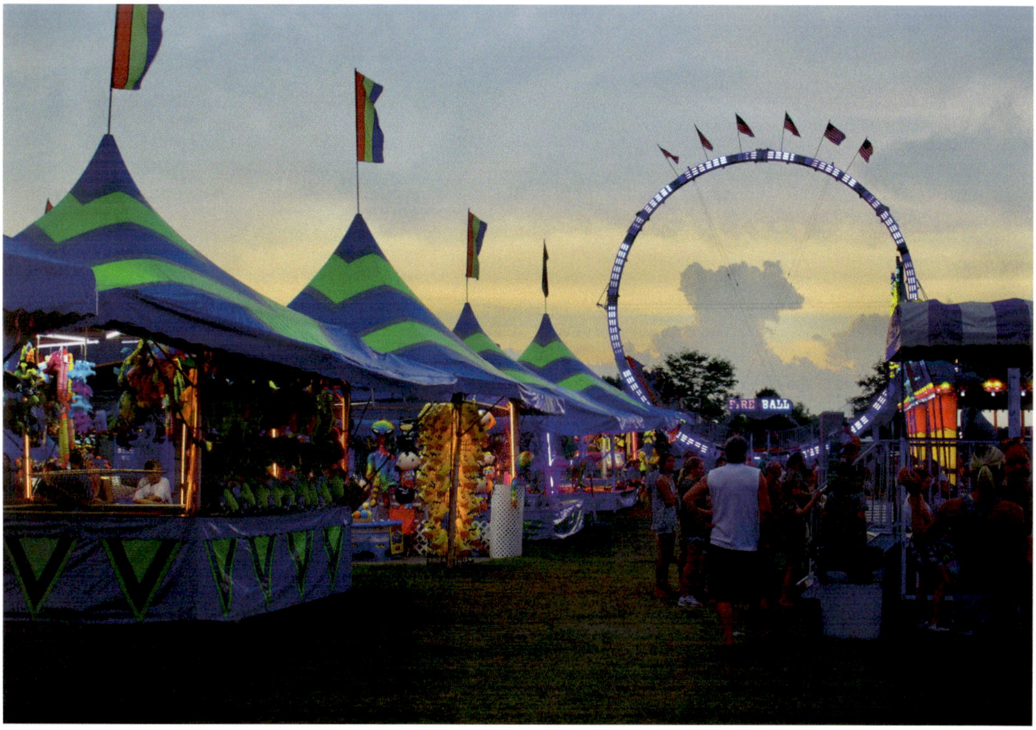

The festive midway draped in bold, vibrant colors at the Goodells 4-H Fair.

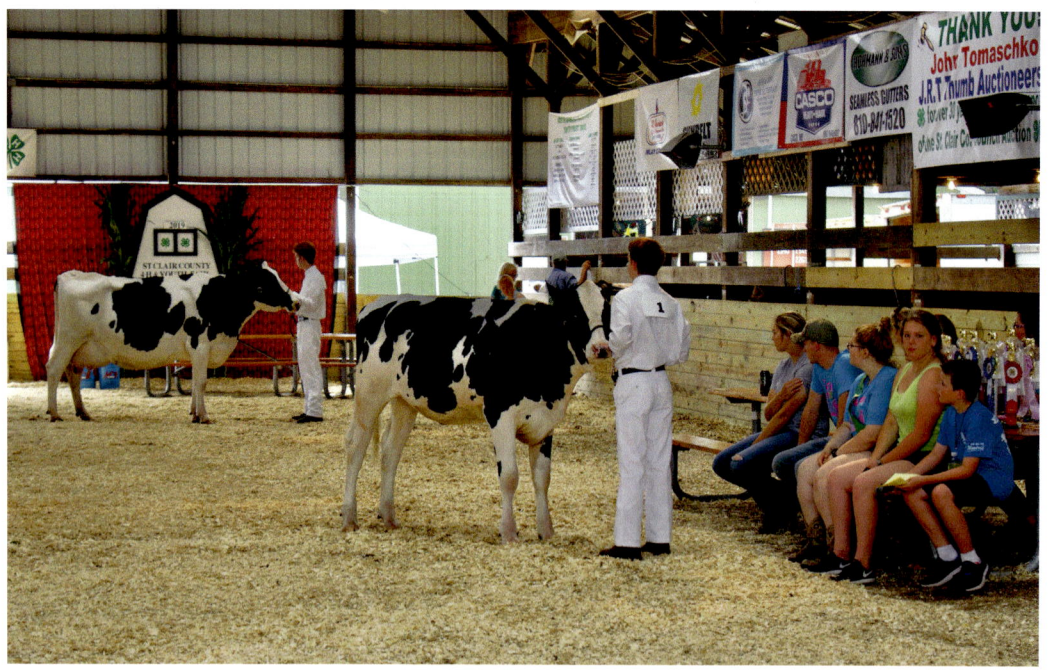

A nervous moment during the dairy cow judging at the county fair.

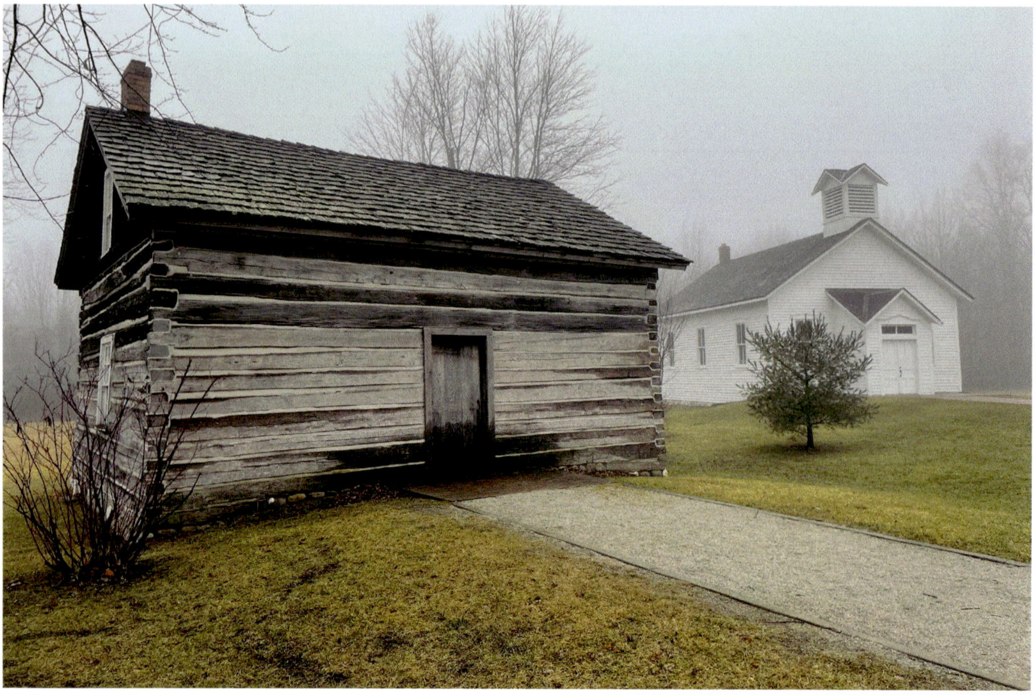

Cloaked in hazy fog, two of the historic buildings at Goodells County Park.

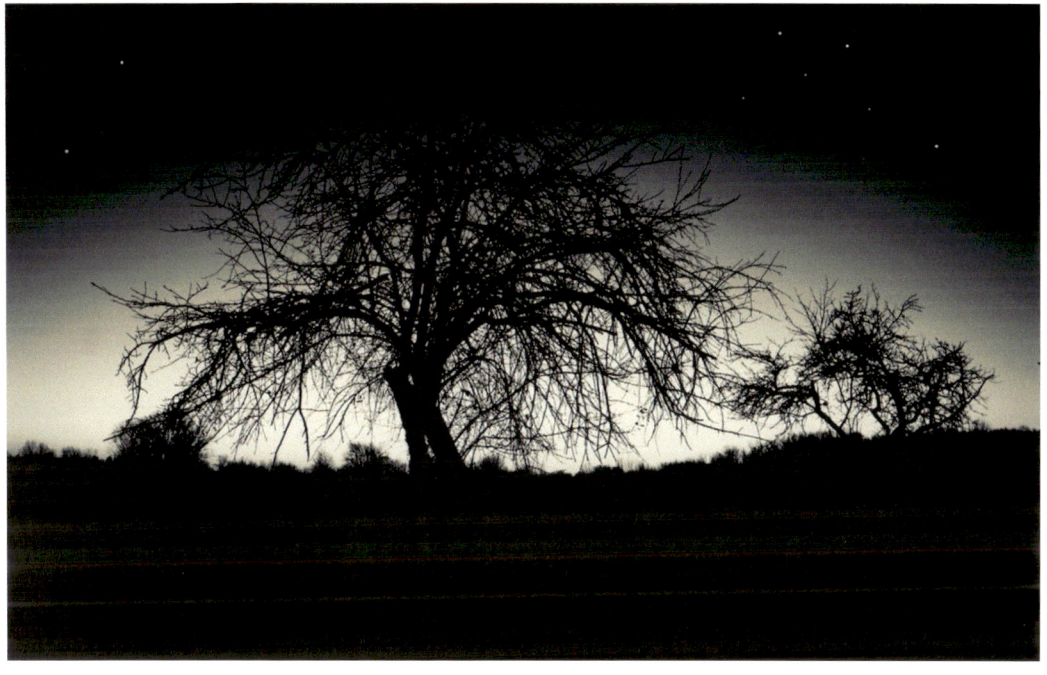

A gnarled tree stands guard at dusk under a starry sky.

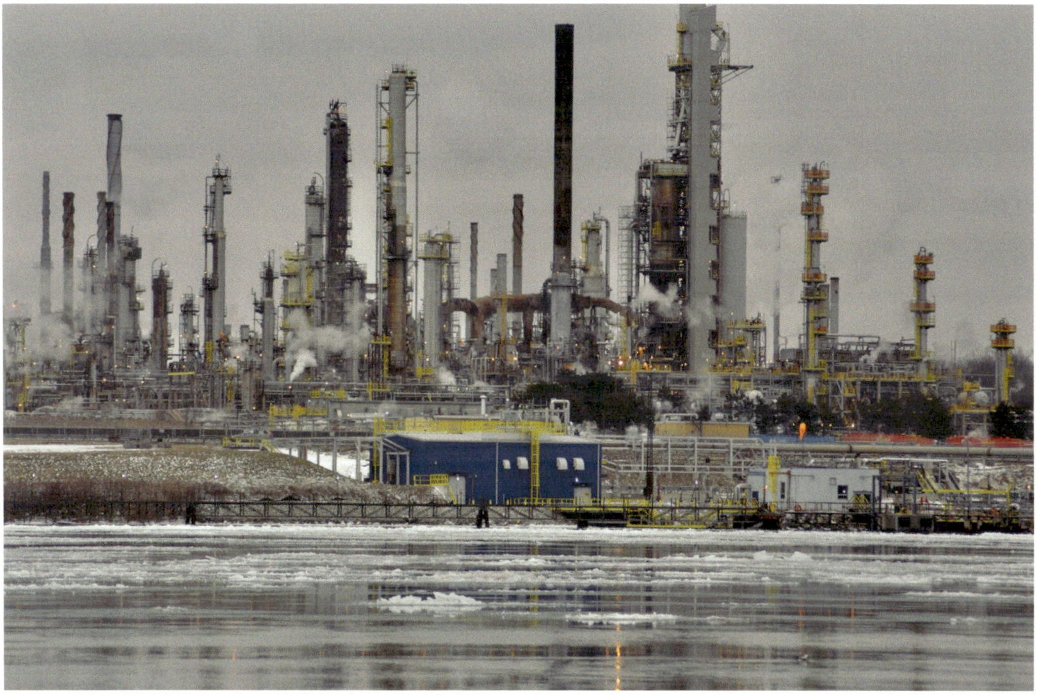

A steely factory in Sarnia, its lights winking to Port Huron from across the icy St. Clair River.

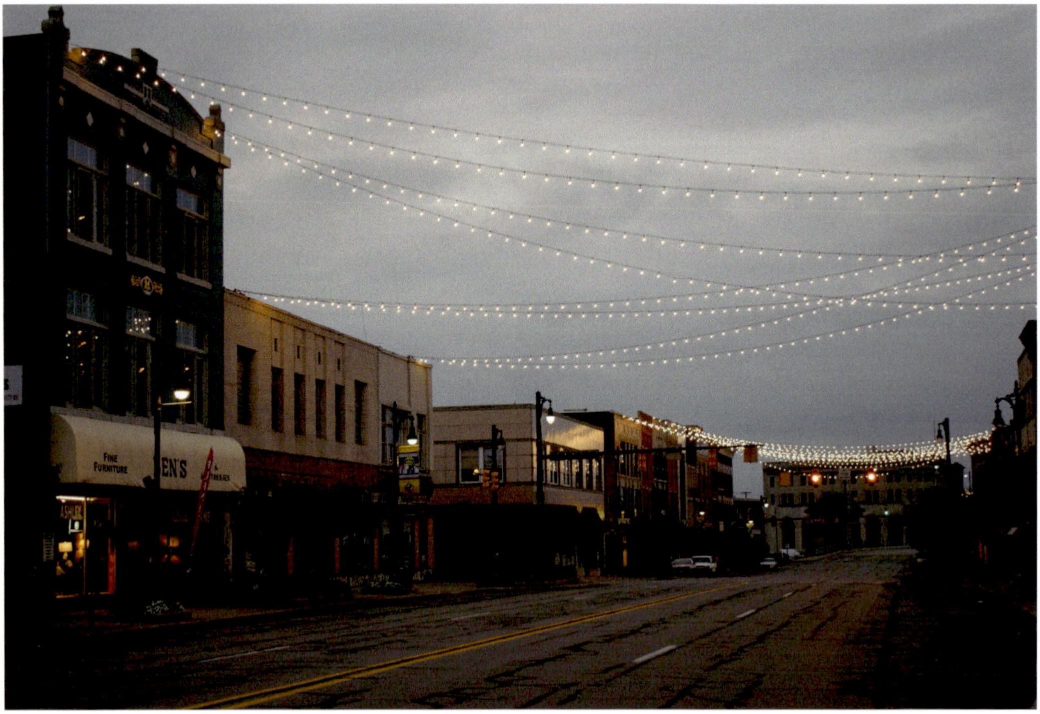

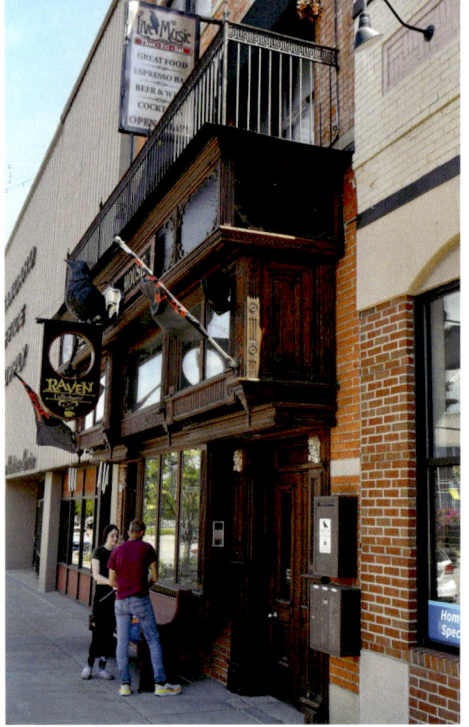

Above: Port Huron's main street through the historic downtown, twinkling with starry lights.

Left: The Raven, an eclectic coffeehouse, the perfect place to have an intellectual chat with friends.

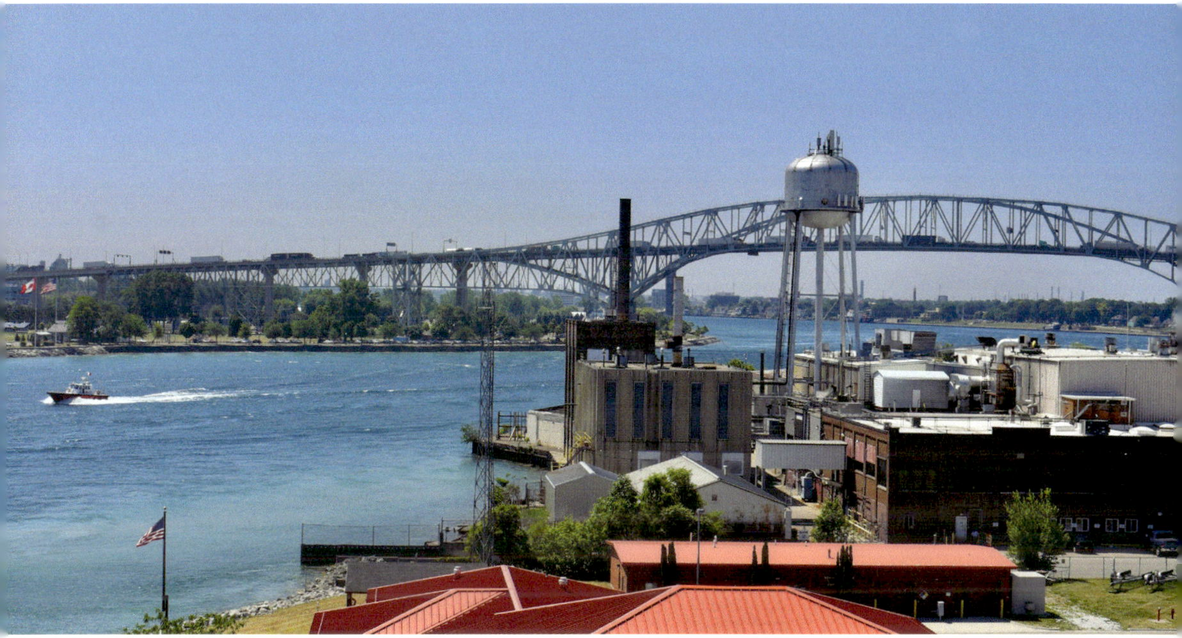

The expansive aquamarine view from the Fort Gratiot Lighthouse in Port Huron, illustrating how the city got the nickname, Blue Water.

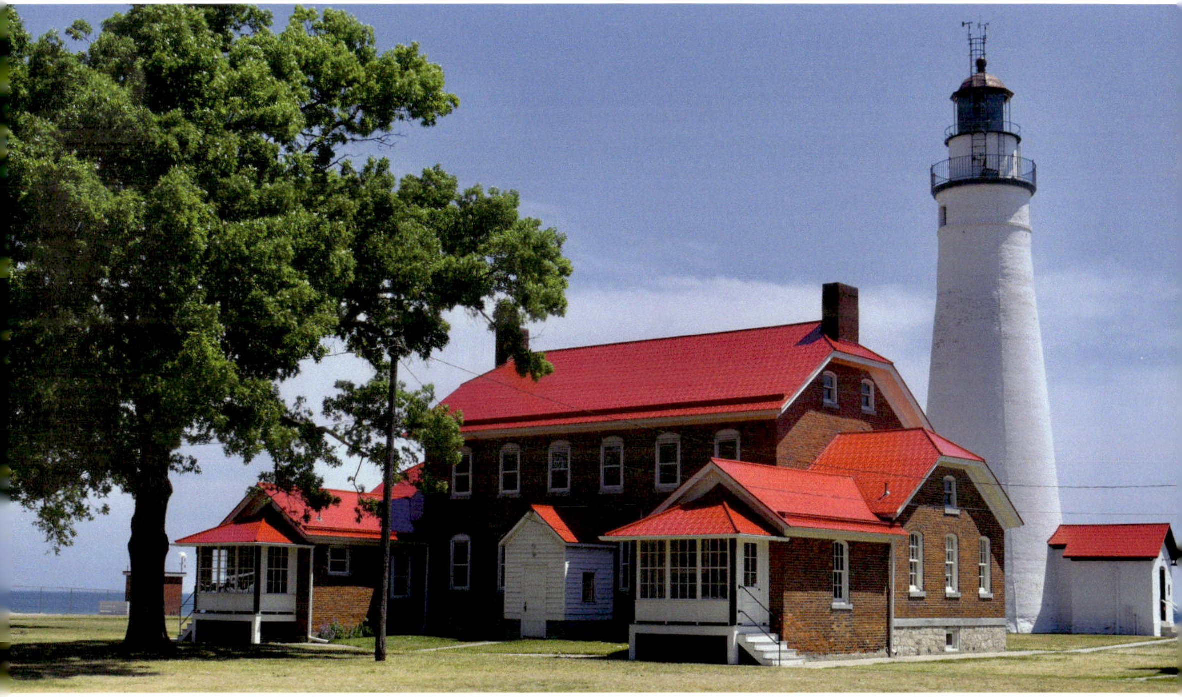

The Fort Gratiot Lighthouse, the oldest lighthouse in Michigan, along with other historic buildings.

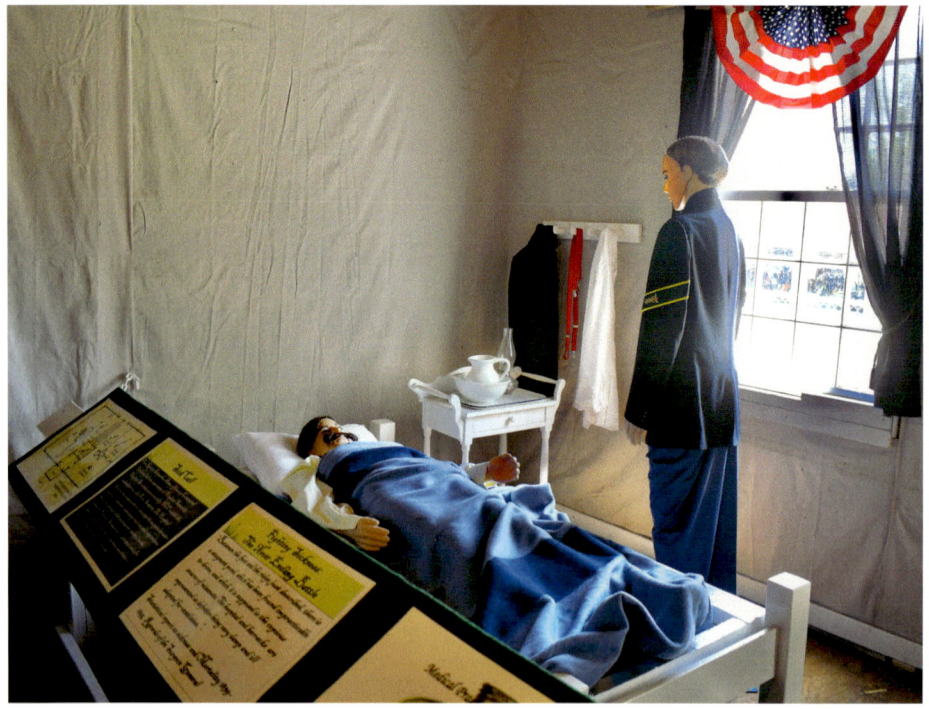

A display from the oldest building in Port Huron, the Fort Gratiot Hospital, built in 1814.

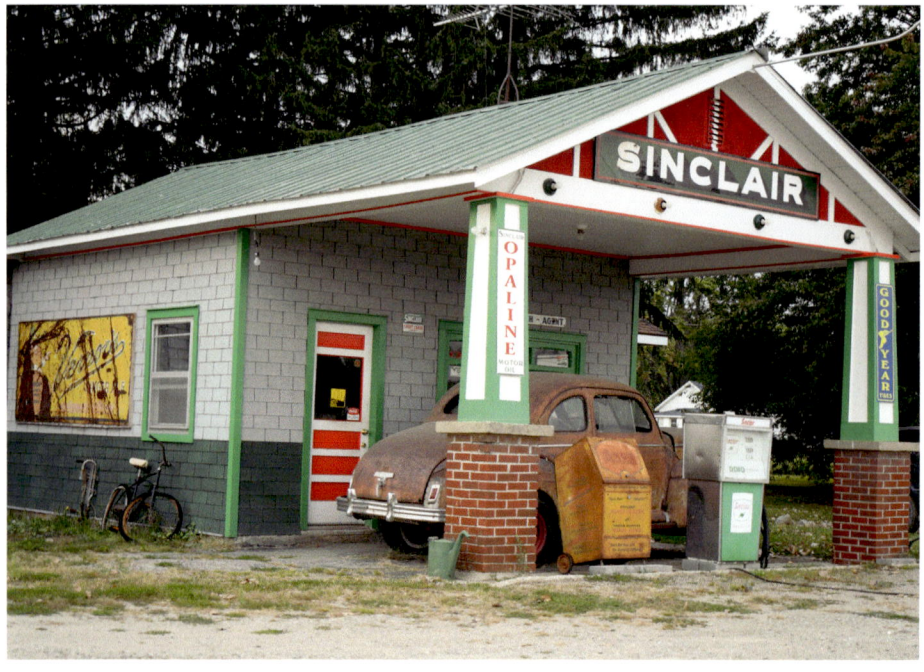

Preserved in time, an old Sinclair gas station in Watertown.

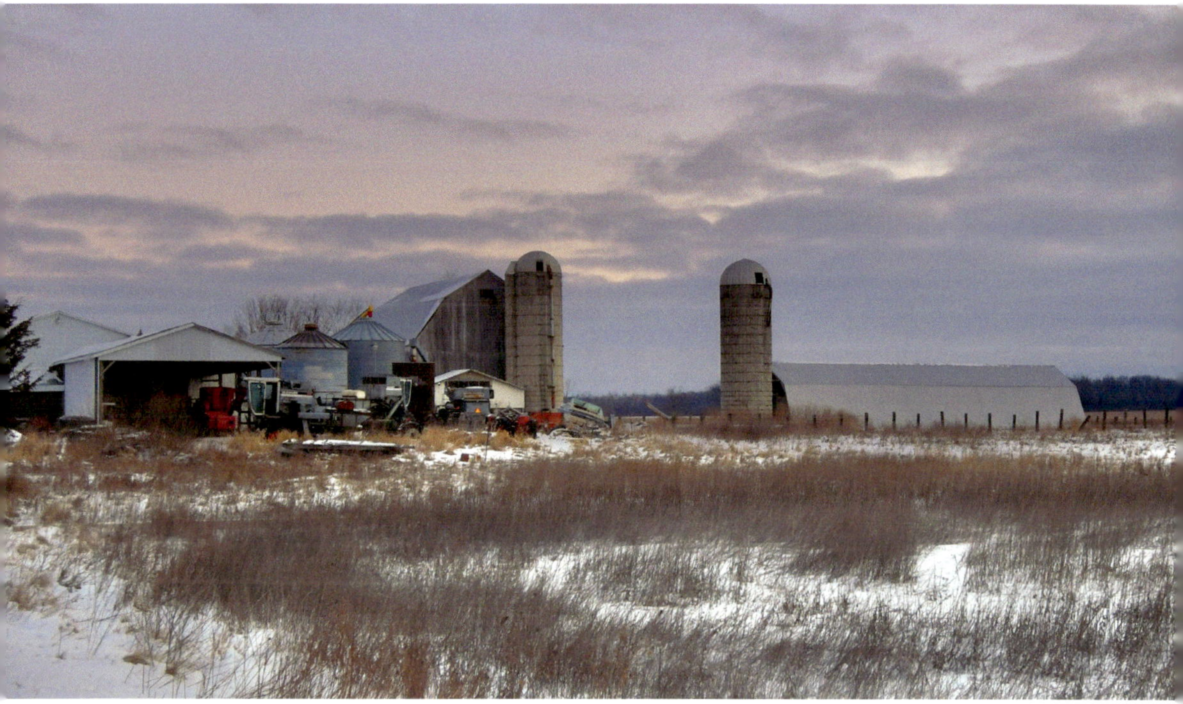

Above: One of the many farmsteads throughout the Thumb, waiting for the warmth of spring.

Right: Lakeport Park in the clutches of winter, its picnic tables lined up like dark soldiers.

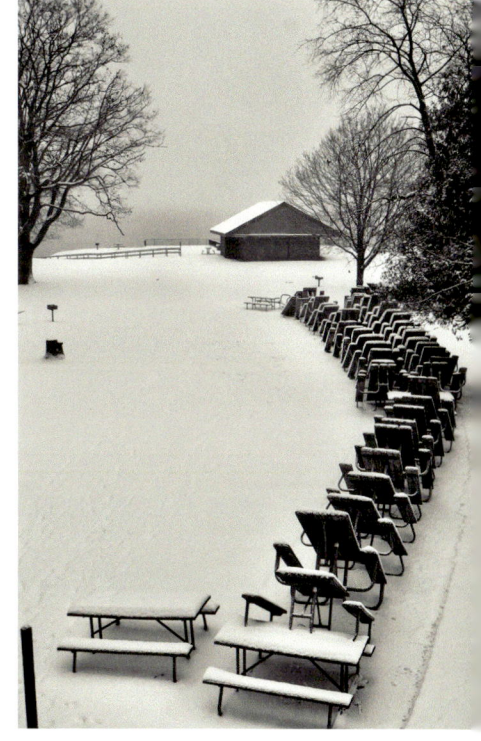

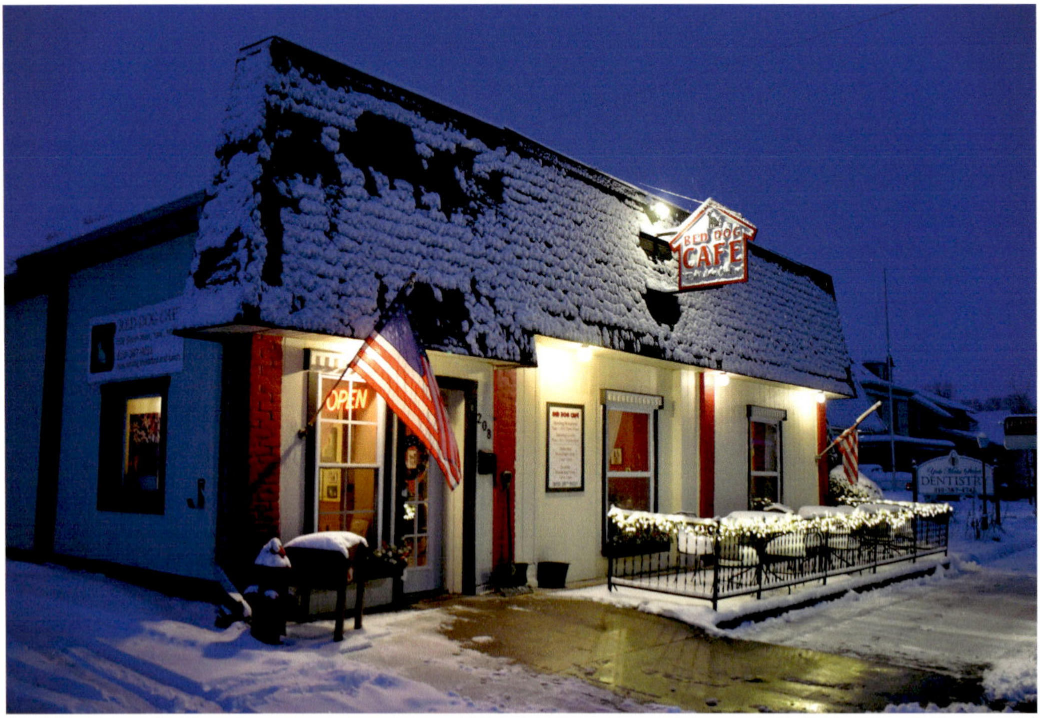

Above: The Red Dog Café in Yale, its warm lights welcoming the hungry breakfast crowd.

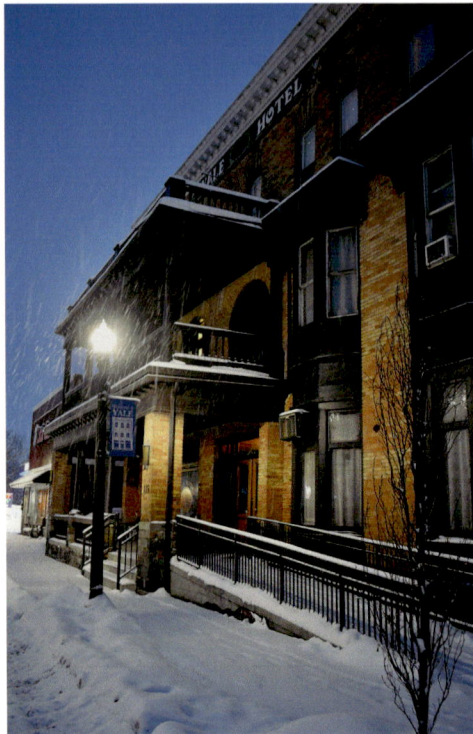

Left: The historic Yale Hotel under soft flakes wafting down from a winter night sky.

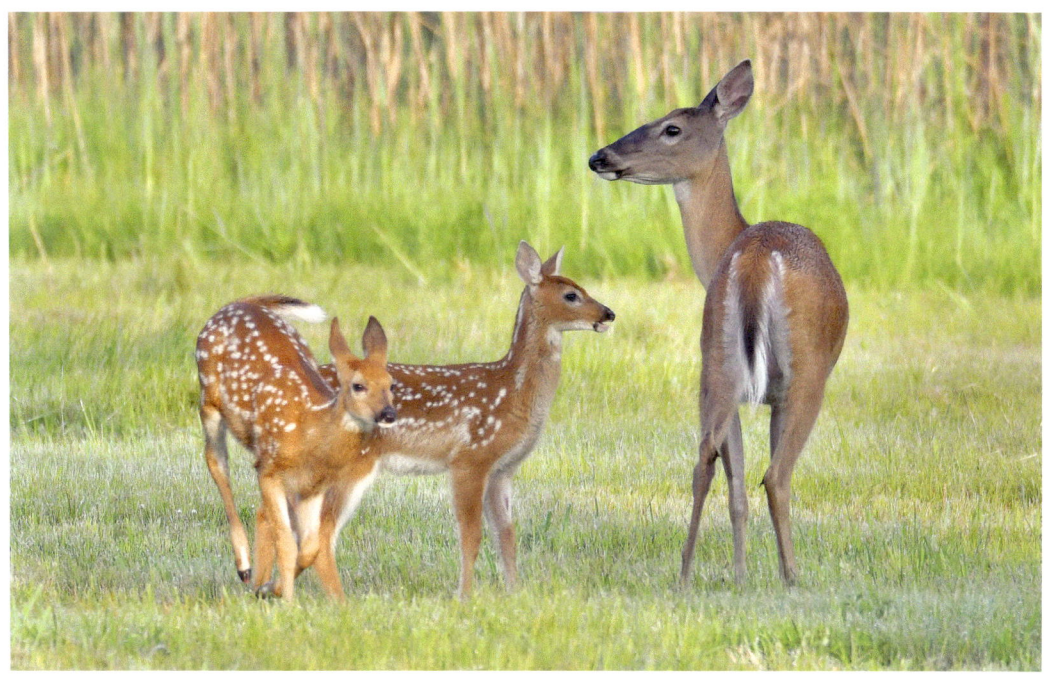

A watchful doe with her frolicking fawns.

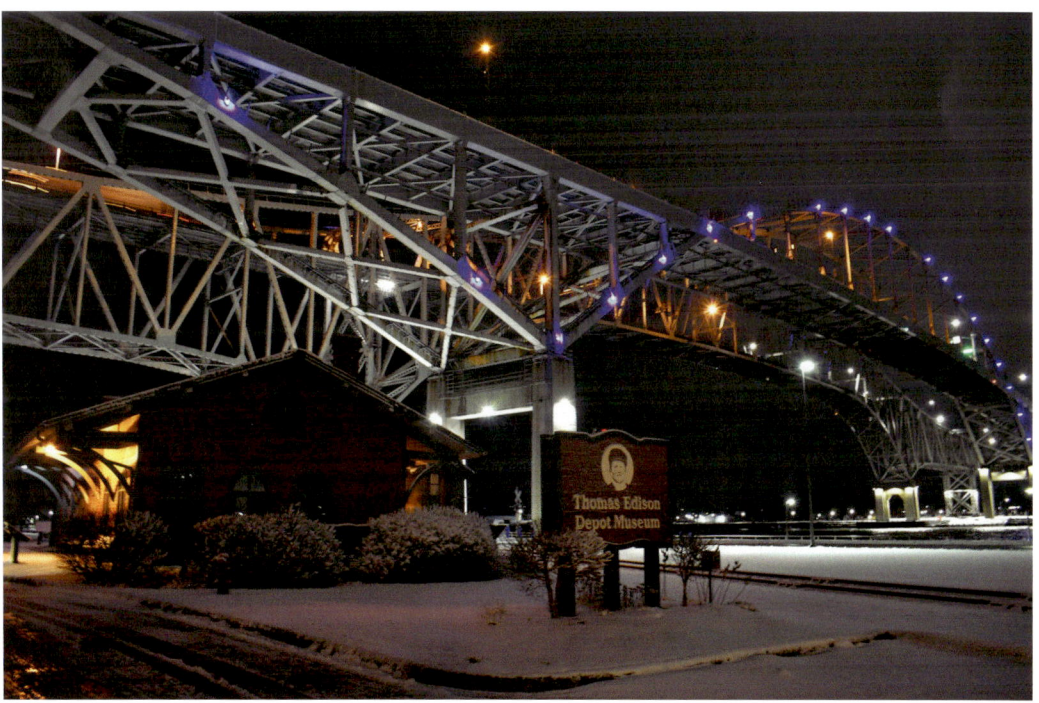

Thomas Edison Museum nestled under the Blue Water Bridge.

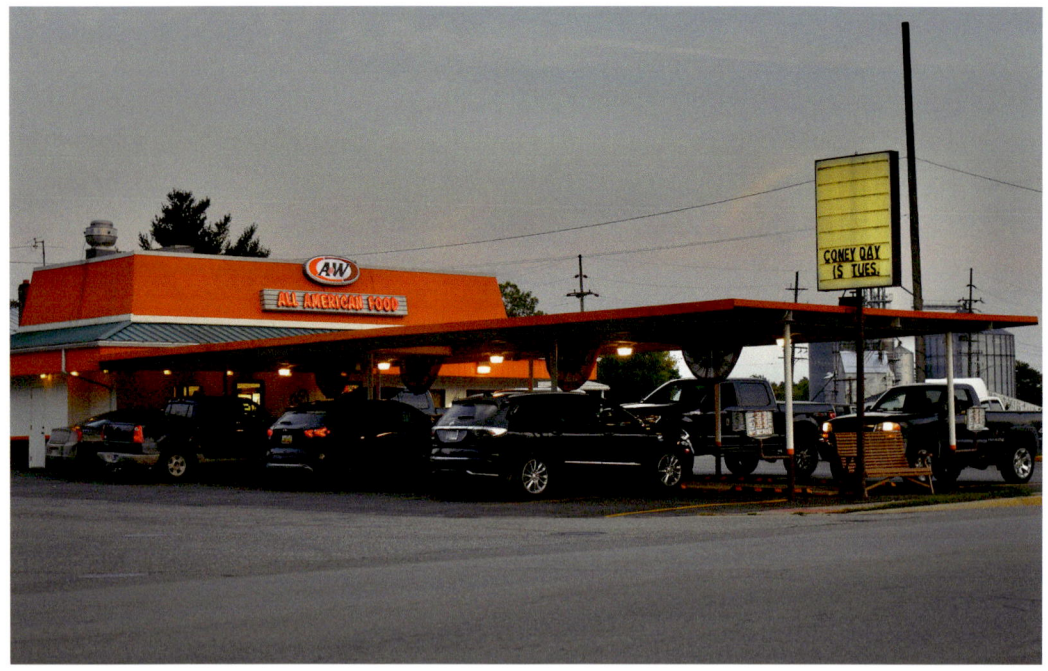

An A & W vintage style drive-in restaurant on a quiet evening in Yale.

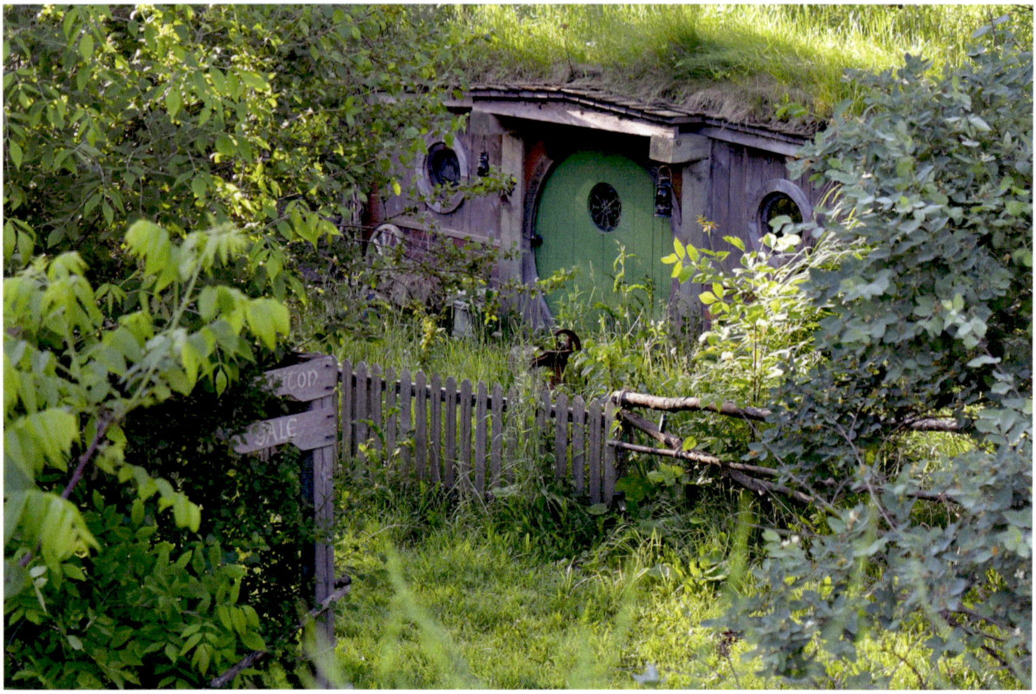

Straight out of a Tolkien novel, a hobbit hole nestled in the bank of a river.

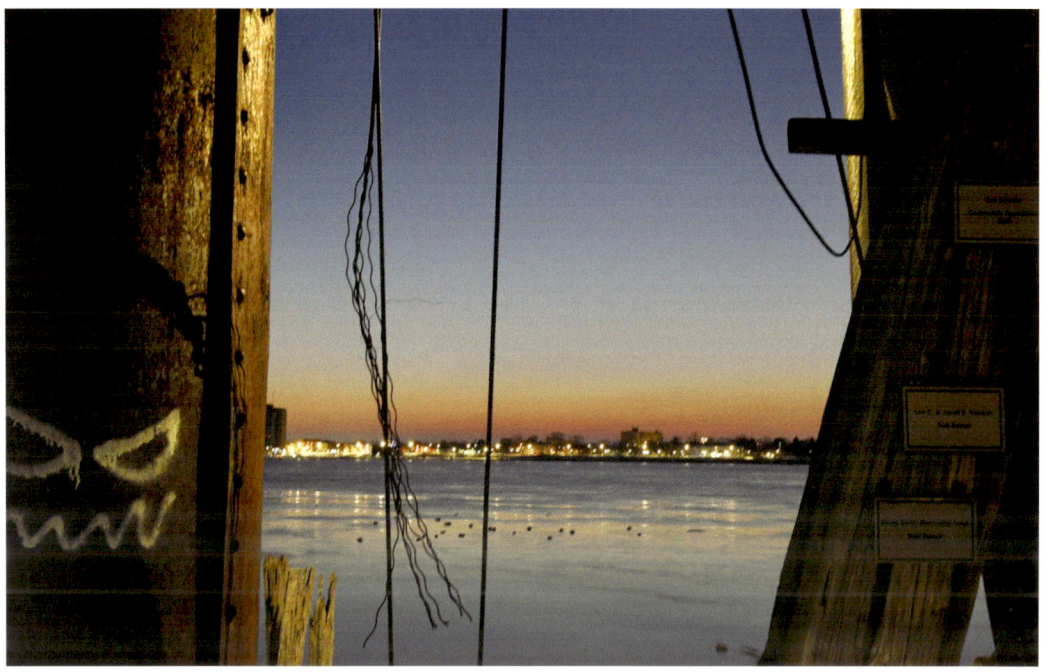

A devious smile frames the St. Clair River.

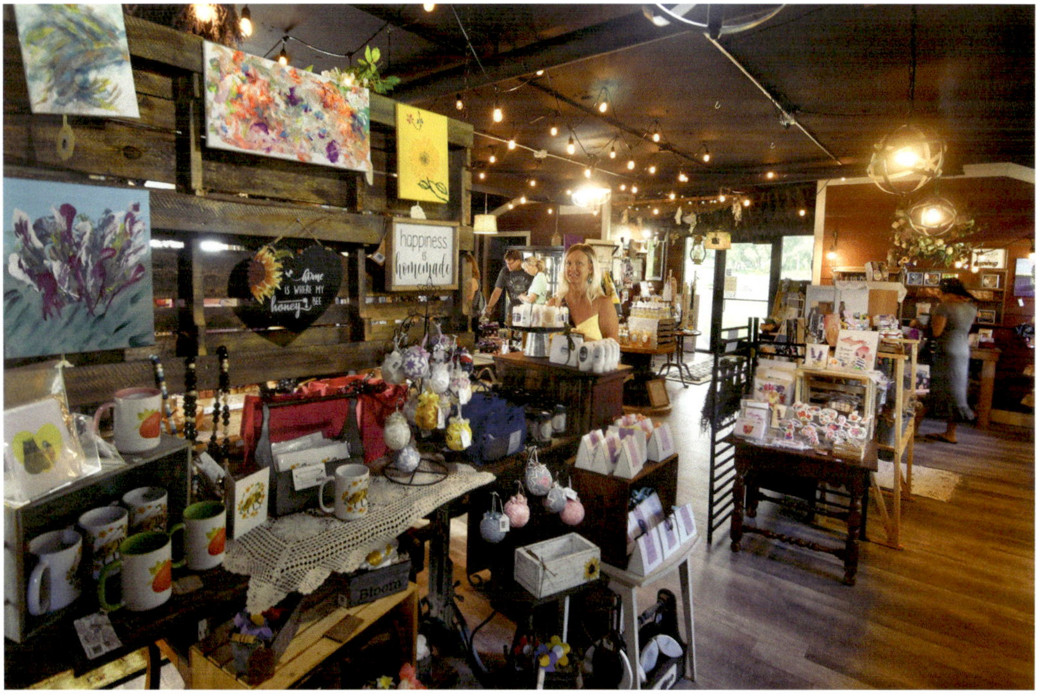

Tempting handicrafts and aromatic gifts in the Indigo Lavender Farms Gift Shop.

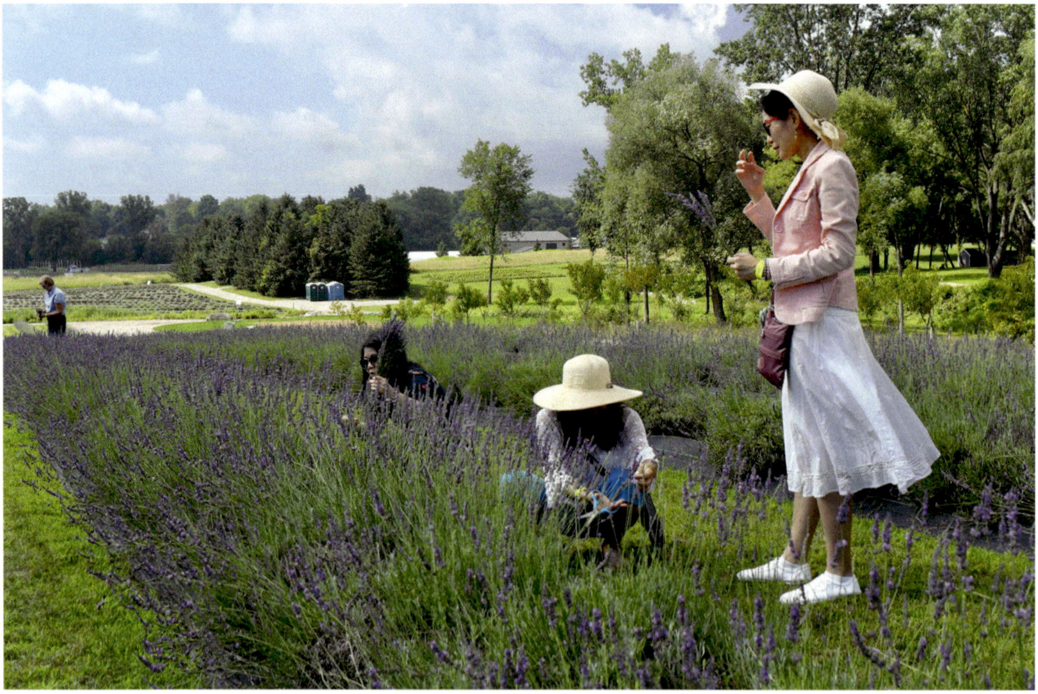

People in the fragrant fields of Indigo Lavender Farms picking purple bouquets.

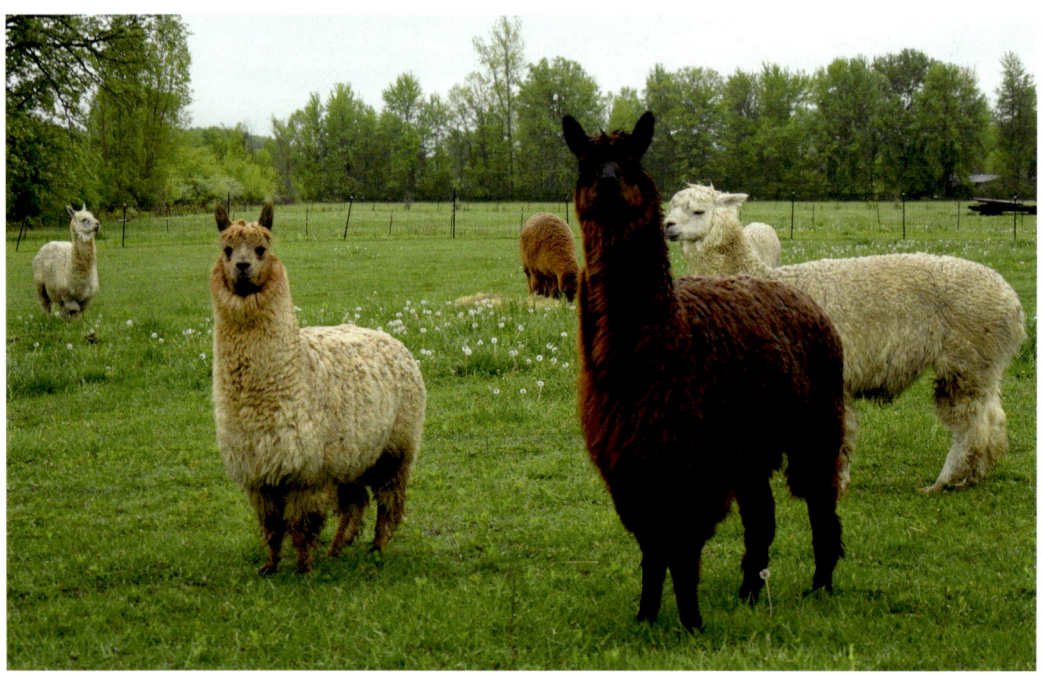

Poofy alpacas enjoying the nippy spring weather.

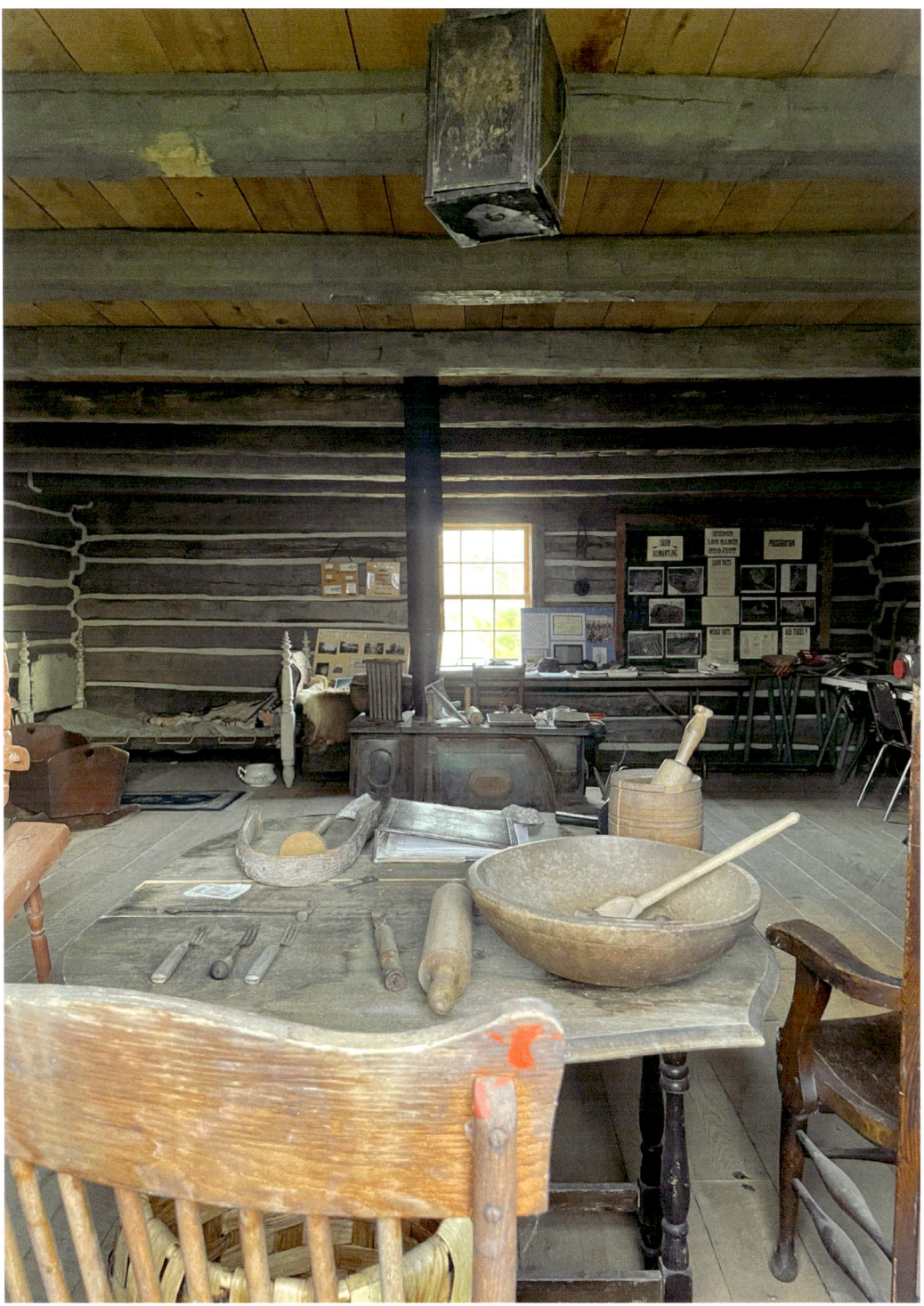

The wooden interior of the notable Mudd log cabin at Goodells County Park.

3

Northwest Region

Frankenmuth is Michigan's Little Bavaria tucked on the west side of the Thumb. Settled in 1845 by a German Lutheran Reverend from Neuendettelsau, who came to convert the Native Americans, the city has features that you would find in an old Bavarian village. Take a walk along Main Street and enjoy the many shops that are sure to satisfy, having goods ranging from handmade beads to delightful fudge to hip garments. Numerous events are hosted year-round, including the Dog Bowl, where canines of all shapes and sizes meet, greet, and sometimes compete, to the Balloons Over Bavarian Inn where brilliant-colored hot air balloons float above the town. The city also has its own brewery with tours, carriage rides, and a waterpark.

Frankenmuth is famous for its homestyle, multiple-dish, chicken dinner. Head to Zehnders at 730 South Main Street, or the Bavarian Inn across the street at 713 South Main Street, to feast on an extravagant dinner almost 100 years in the making. Zehnders' interior is a classic style, with white walls and simple décor while the Bavaria Inn gives a nod to Germany and is decorated in a traditional inn style with wood carvings and vintage beer steins. Head to the basement in Zehnder's to purchase some of the deliciousness you enjoyed above.

To be wrapped in the gaiety of Christmas, head to Bronner's Christmas Wonderland on 25 Christmas Lane, Frankenmuth. Everything you could wish to decorate the home for the holidays is found here. Ornaments with every theme from a tropical island to first responders, hang from the walls, next to trees with glowing lights sparkling with yuletide festivity. Over 50,000 trims and gifts are found across one-and-a-half football fields. Listen to Christmas carols while shopping to your heart's delight.

Saginaw was born from the lumber industry, providing the waterways and tributaries to move cut pine to its sawmills. The boom peaked in the 1870s then collapsed by the end of the century after forests were stripped of their trees. Fur trading was another business that helped build the city in the late 1880s. In the twentieth century, the city again experienced growth with automotive manufacturing plants that helped supply car parts and munitions for World War II. An interesting fact about the city is Stevie Wonder, the singer, and Serena Williams, the tennis star, were both born in Saginaw.

Shiawassee National Wildlife Refuge at 6975 Mower Road, Saginaw, is the place to explore with over 10,000 acres of marsh, grasslands, and bottomland hardwood forests.

With 15 miles of well-marked trails through lush green wetland heavily scented with earthy odors, the area hosts over 280 migratory birds with a chance to see over 100 species of songbirds. Several pairs of eagles nest in the refuge with muskrats, white tail deer, and fox snakes roaming beneath. The refuge is open throughout the year, but trails and roads may be closed due to flooding.

To visit some furry and scaly friends, there is no better place than the Saginaw Children's Zoo located at 1730 Washington Avenue, Saginaw. Part of Celebration Square, a park centered in the heart of the city, the zoo sports a walk-through apiary where birds flutter above, a wetland experience where you can become a beaver, and a hand-carved carousel for a ride on your favorite animal. Resplendent gardens dot the grounds, ladening the air with their fragrance. Kids are sure to love the littlest zoo in Michigan.

For an enchanting experience, head to the Japanese Cultural Center on 527 Ezra Rust Drive, Saginaw. Wander the meticulously designed garden, where each element has a purpose, and nothing crowds each other. View the rock garden where smaller stones symbolize waves breaking on the larger rocks then head to the Japanese gazebo. For the ultimate immersive experience, have tea in the teahouse, where not a single nail was used in its creation. The grounds were established as a friendship bridge between Saginaw and its sister city, Tokushima in Japan.

On the grounds of Saginaw State University at 7400 Bay Road, University Center, is the Marshall M. Fredericks Sculpture Museum. Marshall is one of the most notable sculptors of the twentieth century. His work is found in over 150 spots in the United States and can also be viewed overseas in countries such as Japan and Denmark. When you enter the museum, a warm glow illuminates 200 of his ivory figures and creatures, which dance and contort in smooth, curvaceous lines. Head outside, where tarnished bronze Frederick's statues loll in a bubbling fountain.

Located on the western side of the Thumb is Bay City, cut in half by the rolling Saginaw River. The city was once known as the "Lumber Capital of the World" and has a rich history dating back to 1837. What spurred the city's growth was the booming lumber industry which spurred affluent and influential people from all over to flock to the area. Magnificent lumber barons' mansions still line the city's Center Avenue highlighting an age when cut wood flowed money into everyone's coffers. The beautiful architecture around the downtown is all that remains of a once thriving industry.

Go back in time and walk down Center Avenue, Bay City, which is a part of the Bay City Center Avenue Historic District. Dozens of mansions more than 100 years old from lumber tycoons line the boulevard and the nearby surrounding neighborhood. Some of the houses date back more than 150 years. A wide array of styles can be found including Gothic Revival, Queen Anne, Tudor Revival, and Italianate. Two of the more notable are the Frederick E. Bradley house at 1000 Center Avenue and the John Knaggs house at 813 N. Sheridan Street. Bradley was the brother of the first mayor of Bay city while the Knaggs residence once hosted Susan B. Anthony.

Sporting the crimsons and golds of a glorious sunset is the Delta College Planetarium at 100 Center Avenue, Bay City. The building's design is meant to mimic the solar city. The theater is located at the center of the building just as the sun is at the center of the solar system. The theater's outside recreates a rocket exhaust nozzle. When entering the building, you are taken in an elliptical path around the interior, as if you were one of the planets circling the sun. There are only spherical windows, like planets in the sky. The theater has a 360-dome viewing screen so you may experience the universe in all its glory.

Built in 1908, the State Theater at 913 Washington Avenue, Bay City, heralds from the days of vaudeville and burlesque houses. Decorated with a Mayan theme resembling an archaic pyramid, the theater's colorful facade stares back at you from the neon eyes of an ancient glowing god. Inside, the interior is softly lit and takes you back to the 1930s with polished brick covering its walls and surrounding its stage as if you walked into an actual pyramid.

The Saginaw Valley Naval Ship Museum at 1680 Martin Street, Bay City, rests in the bowels of the USS *Edson*, a retired United States Navy destroyer from 1958 which was used for combat in the Vietnam War. Immerse yourself in the history of the Navy while walking on the ship's deck as it floats in the Saginaw River. Peer inside to experience what it felt like for sailors who served on the vessel as 90% of the interior is open for a self-guided tour, including the wheelhouse where the commander steered the ship.

If you love the wail of the siren of a fire engine, you won't want to miss Antique Toy and Firehouse Museum at 3456 Patterson Road, Bay City, home to over sixty motorized fire engines, including the workhorse FDNY Super Pumper, which could draw from eight fire hydrants at once with a 10,000-gallon-per-minute flow. The museum also contains one of the largest collections of toy trucks, with many first responder vehicles and fire apparatus.

Sink your teeth into some fried, sugary deliciousness at Cops and Donuts, Sutherland Precinct, located at 710 East Midland Street, Bay City. An offshoot of the Cops and Donuts in Clare, which was saved from closing its doors by the nine police officers of the city, the business is set in the historic Sutherland Bakery from 1912. Stop by for delectable donuts and scrumptious pastries washed down with some fresh-brewed coffee.

Have a sweet tooth? Then check out the Michigan Sugar Factory Tour at 2600 South Euclid Avenue in Bay City. Built in 1901, the factory is just one of Pioneer Big Chief's factories that are scattered across the Thumb region. The tours are hosted during the processing of the sugar beets, and Bay City produces over 440 million pounds of sugar alone. The tour lasts an hour and involves a mile of walking. It is a wonderful way to learn about an industry from the area, which employs many Thumb residents.

Step back in time 100 years and catch a glimpse of the rural life at the Thumb Octagon Barn Agricultural Museum. Located at 6948 Richie Road, Gagetown, the museum is one of the numerous buildings on 40 acres, including an extravagant fifteen-room home, sawmill, grain elevator, blacksmith shop, one-room schoolhouse, cider mill, and sugar shack. Pet friendly farm animals, view apples being pressed into golden cider, marvel at the making of maple syrup, or stroll through the renovated buildings filled with antiques and vintage pieces from the past. The site hosts numerous festivals from flea markets to ice cream socials.

Bay Port Fish Company, started in 1895, located at 1008 1st Street, Bay Port, is one of the thirteen remaining commercial fisheries in the state, where there used to be thousands. With their three vessels, the fishery hauls in fresh fish every day seasonally, including whitefish, cod, walleye, and trout, which is available for purchase at their store along with frozen and smoked fish. The company also supplies the Fish Sandwich Festival in Bay Port in August with fish caught by local fisherman.

The Strand Theater, at 101 South State Street in Caro, is a single-screen theater from the 1920s, its colorful facade in the art deco style lit by tubes of neon. Playing first-run movies, the theater, which was renovated in the 1990s, provides a charming place for a night out in this small town.

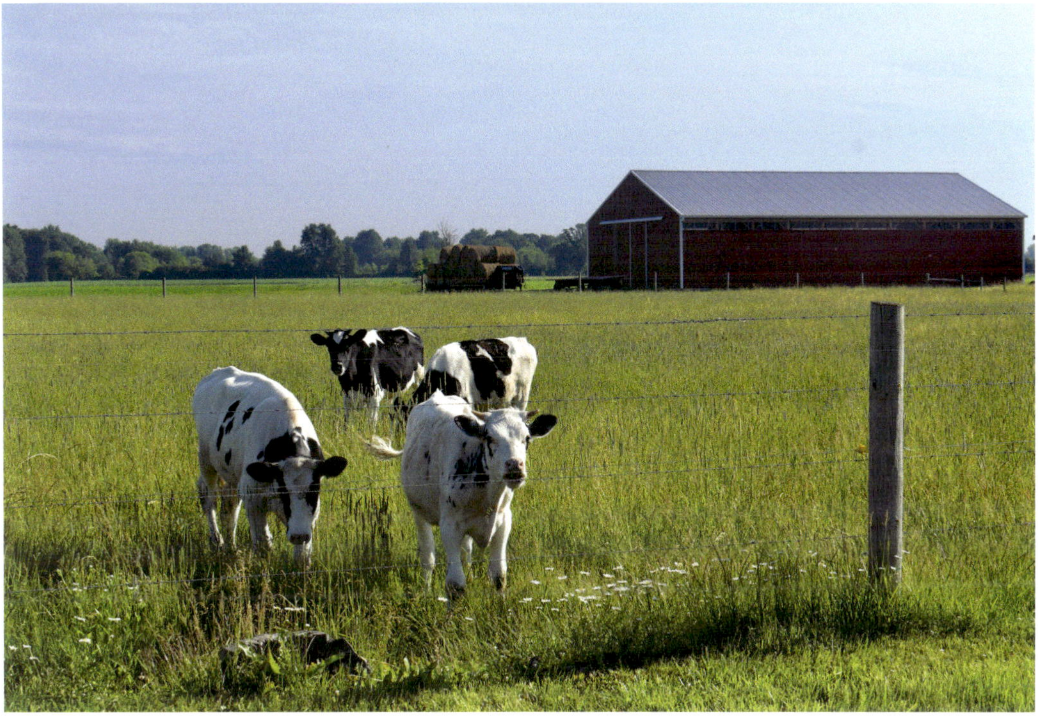

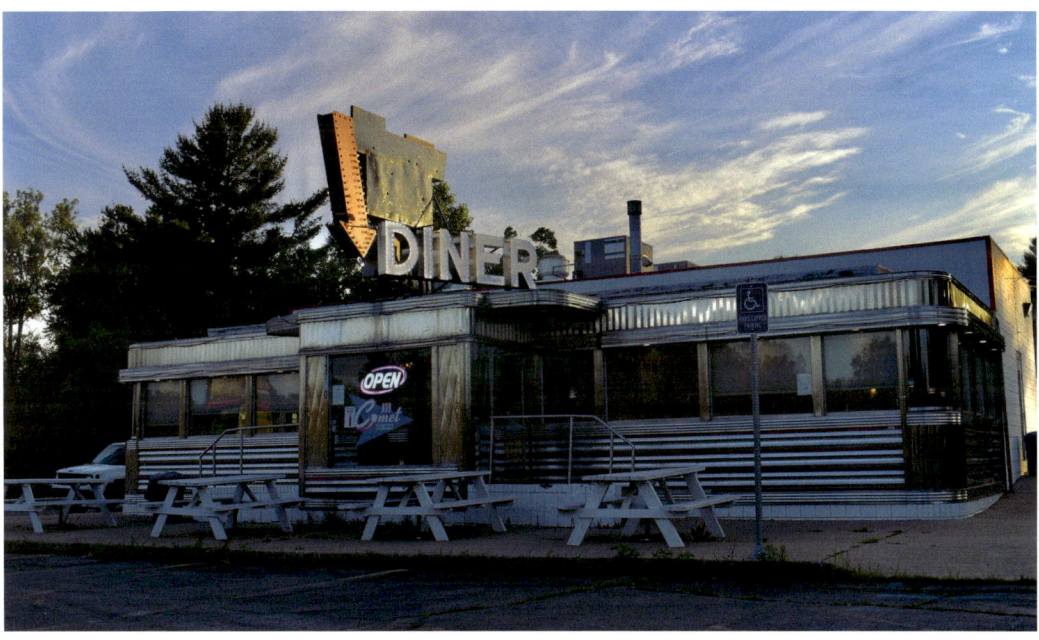

A small herd of young, curious cows nibbling on summer pasture.

The Comet Classic Diner in Birch Run serving up plates of crispy fries with sizzling burgers.

A young woman clowns around at Bronner's Christmas Wonderland.

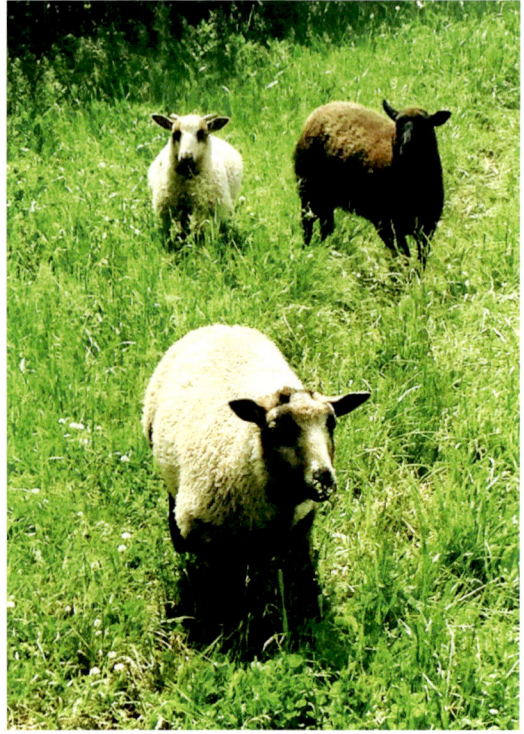

Young sheep amble through an emerald spring pasture.

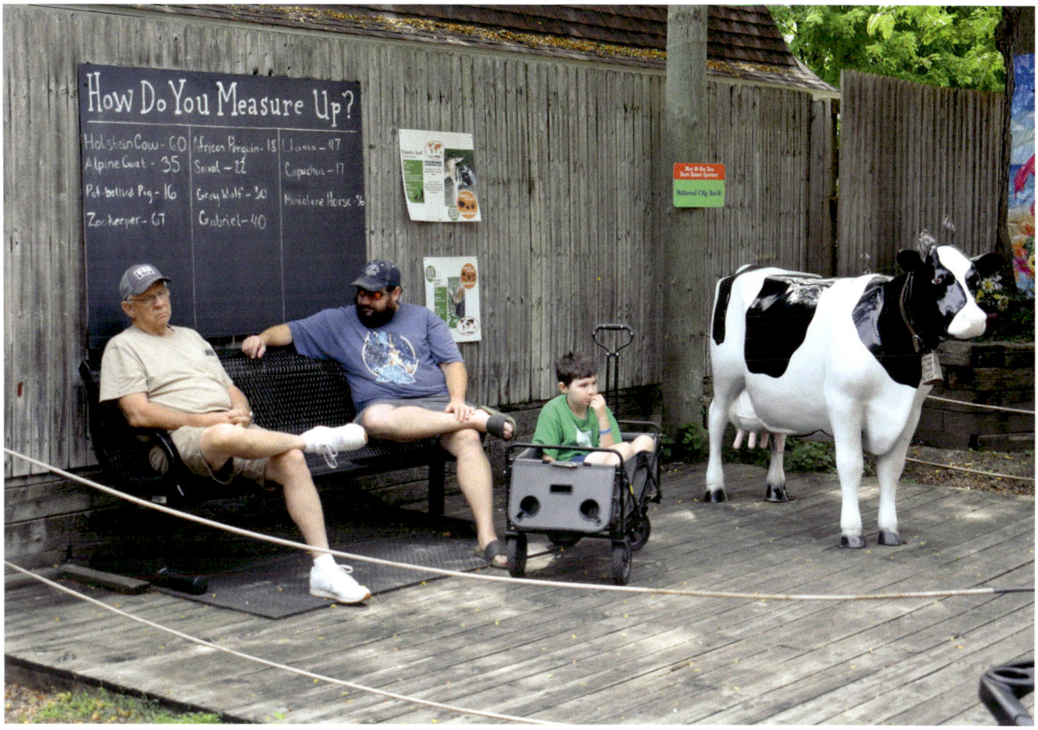

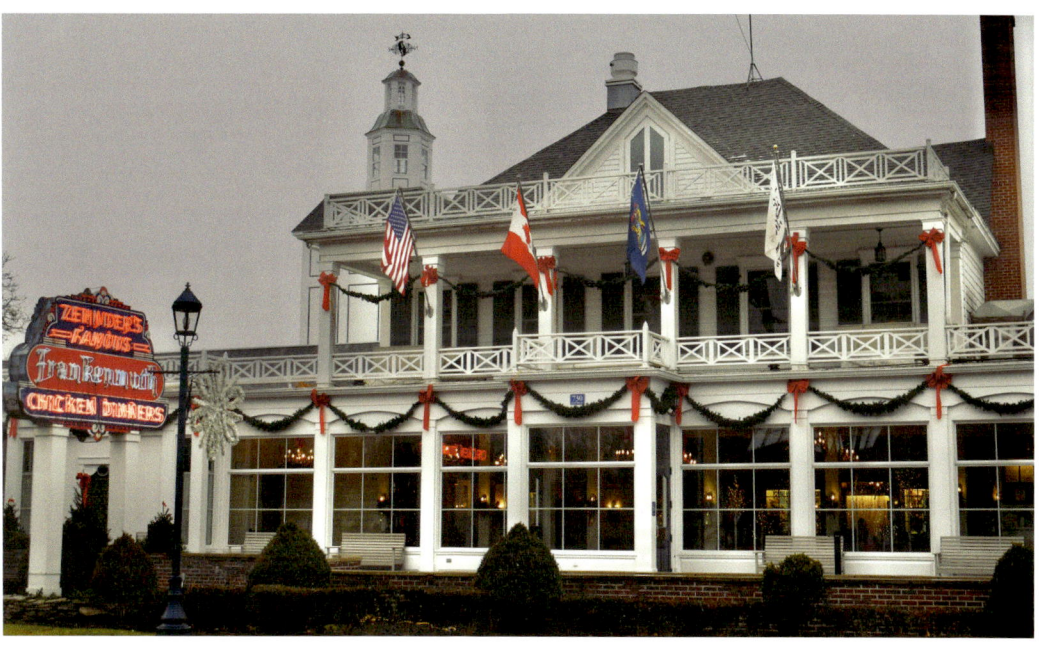

Taking a break on a hot steamy day at the Saginaw Children's Zoo.

The stately Zehnder's in Frankenmuth decked with flags under a sooty evening sky.

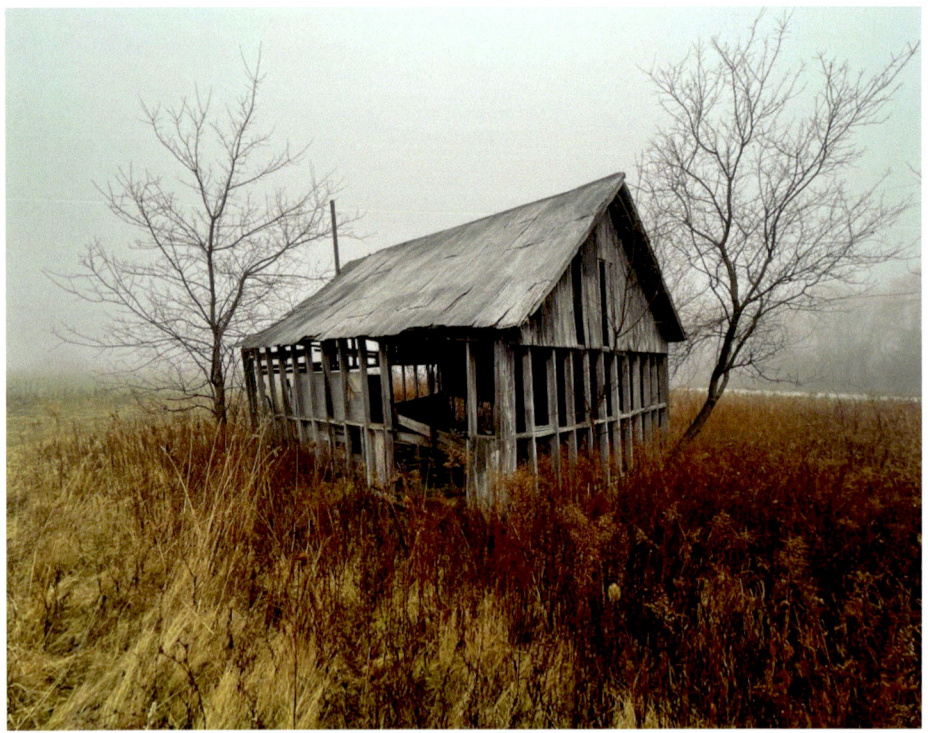

An old shed shrouded in fog, one of the many thumb structures made with hand-cut wood.

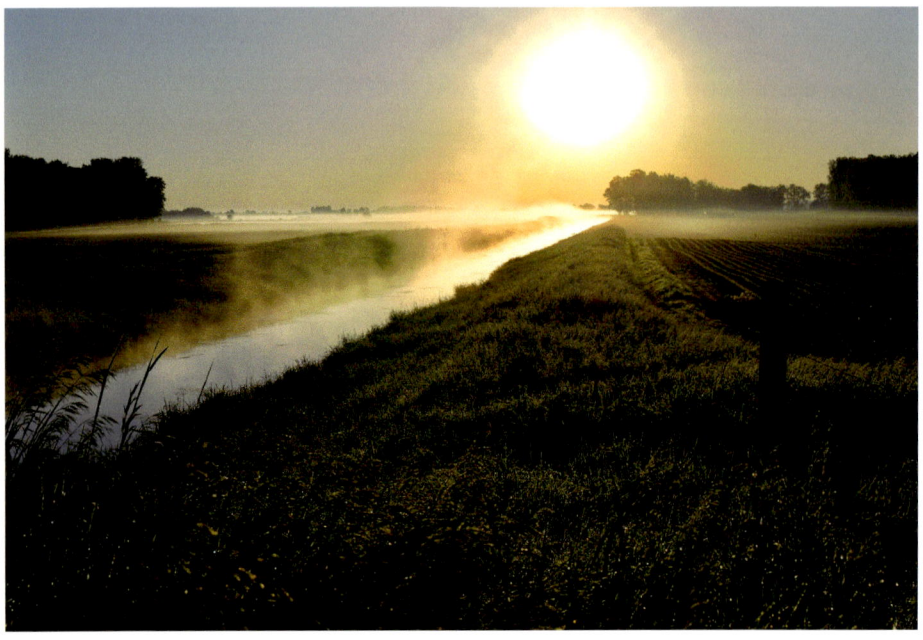

Misty clouds rolling over a fertile field in the Thumb.

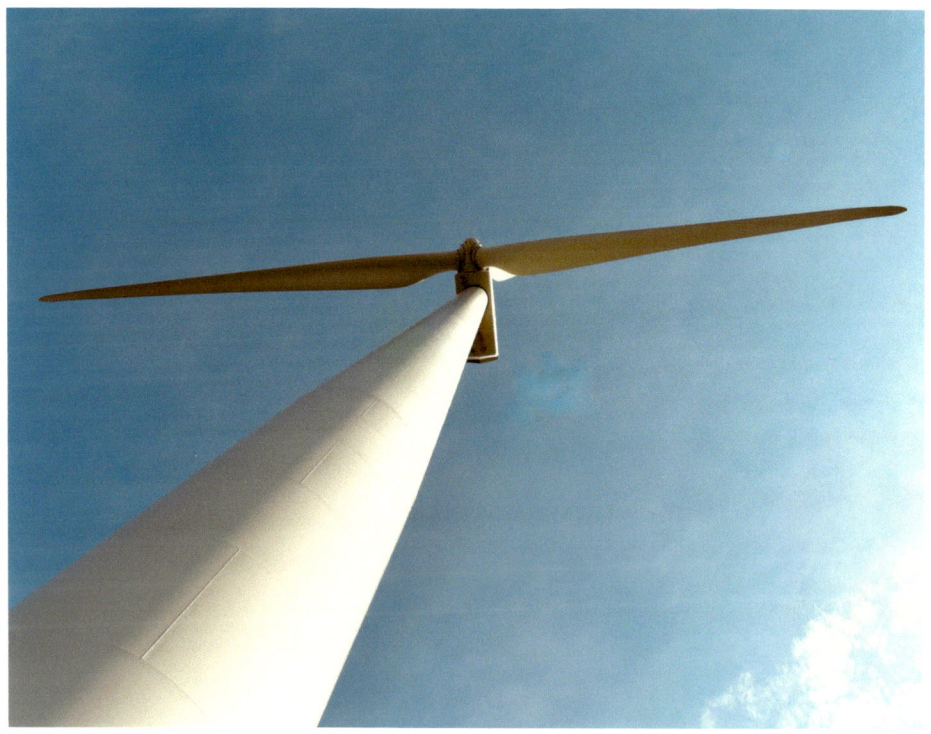

Gazing up at a wind turbine, a familiar sight in the Thumb region.

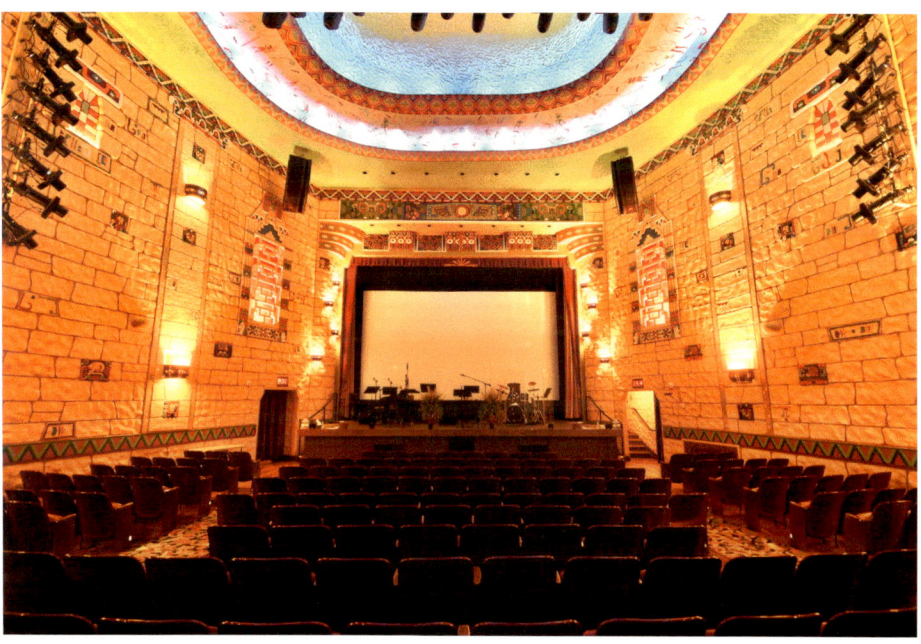

The luminous, bricked interior of the 1908 State Theater in Bay City.

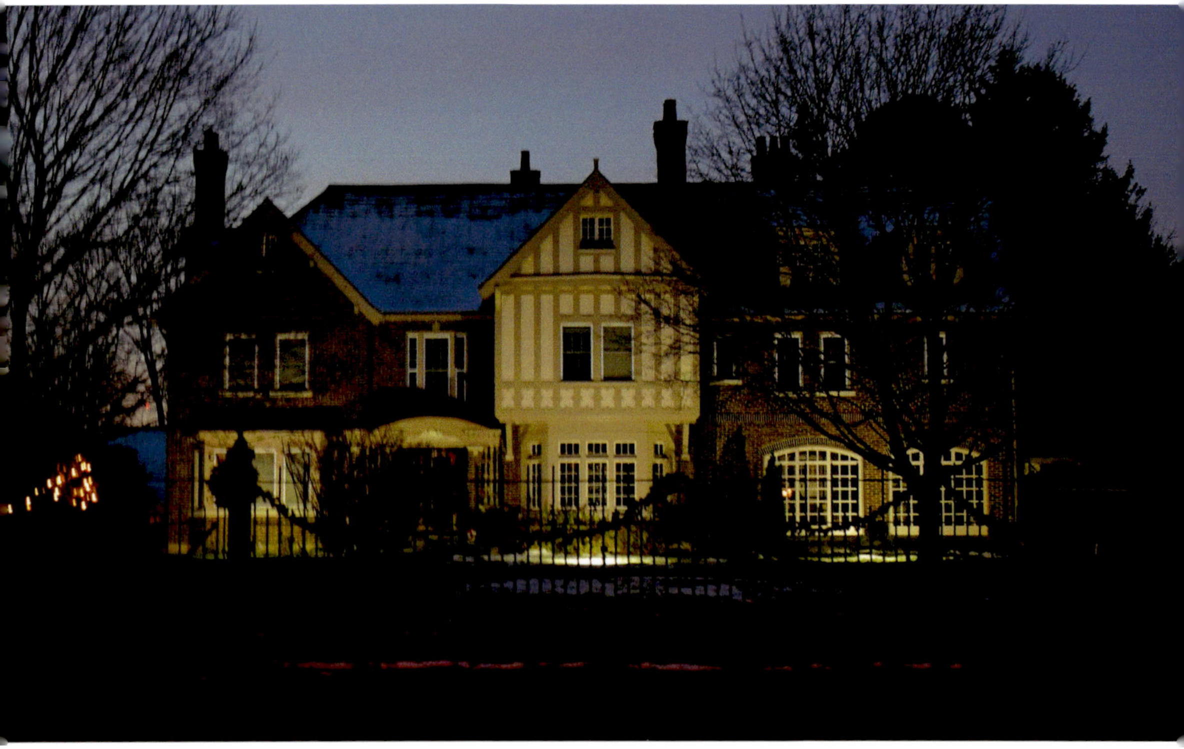

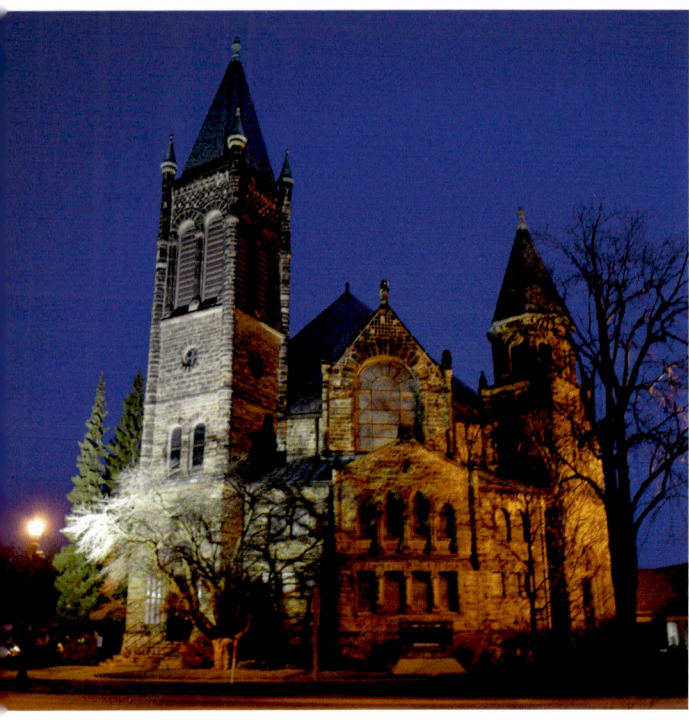

Above: One of the mansions from the lumber barons' era on Center Avenue in Bay City.

Left: The hauntingly beautiful First Presbyterian Church in Bay City from 1893.

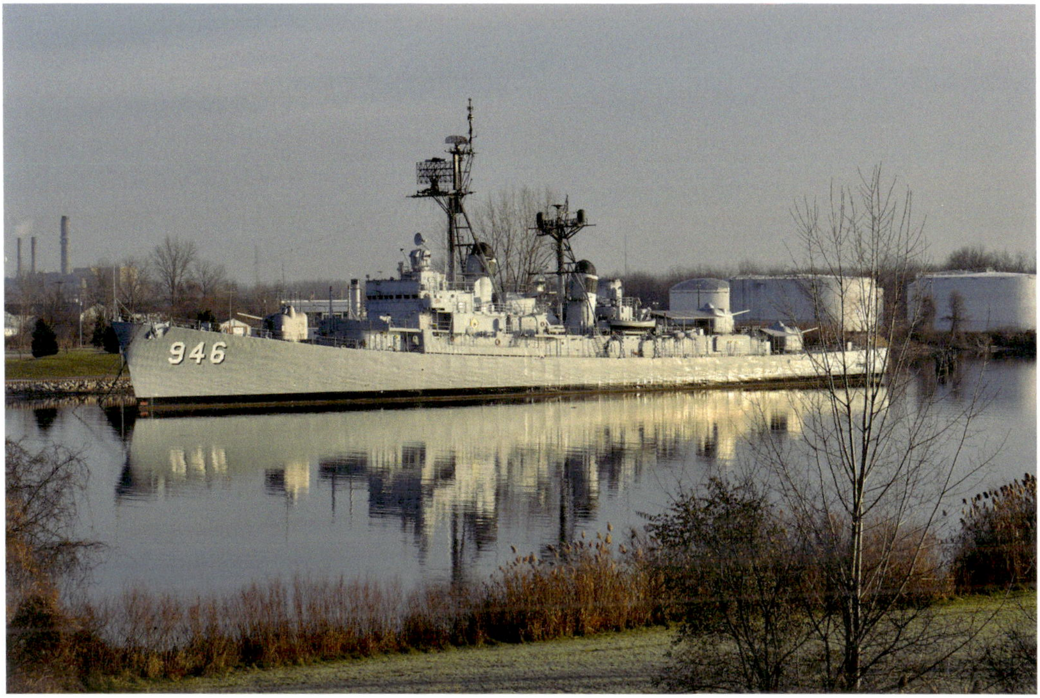

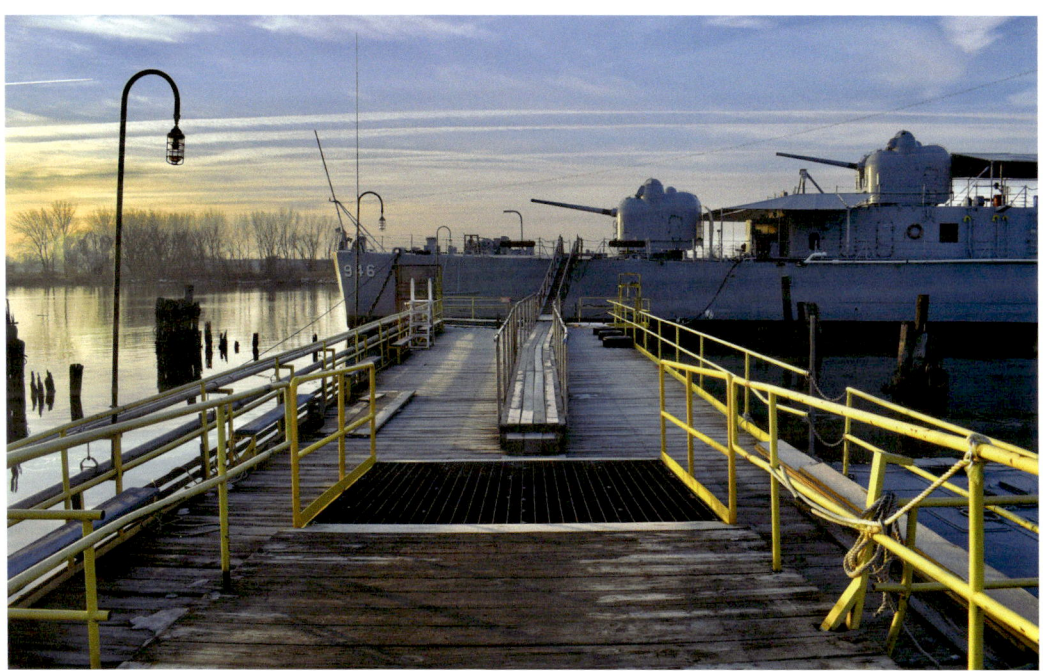

The majestic USS *Edson*, location of the Saginaw Valley Naval Ship Museum.

The USS *Edson* Saginaw Valley Naval Ship Museum illuminated by the yellow rays of daybreak.

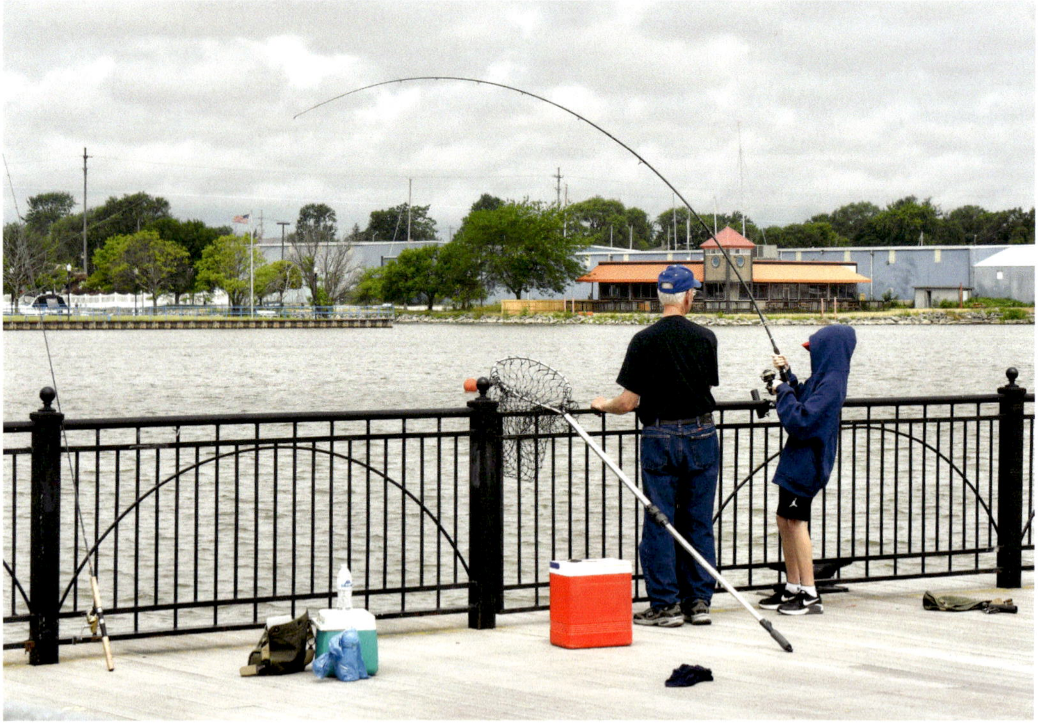

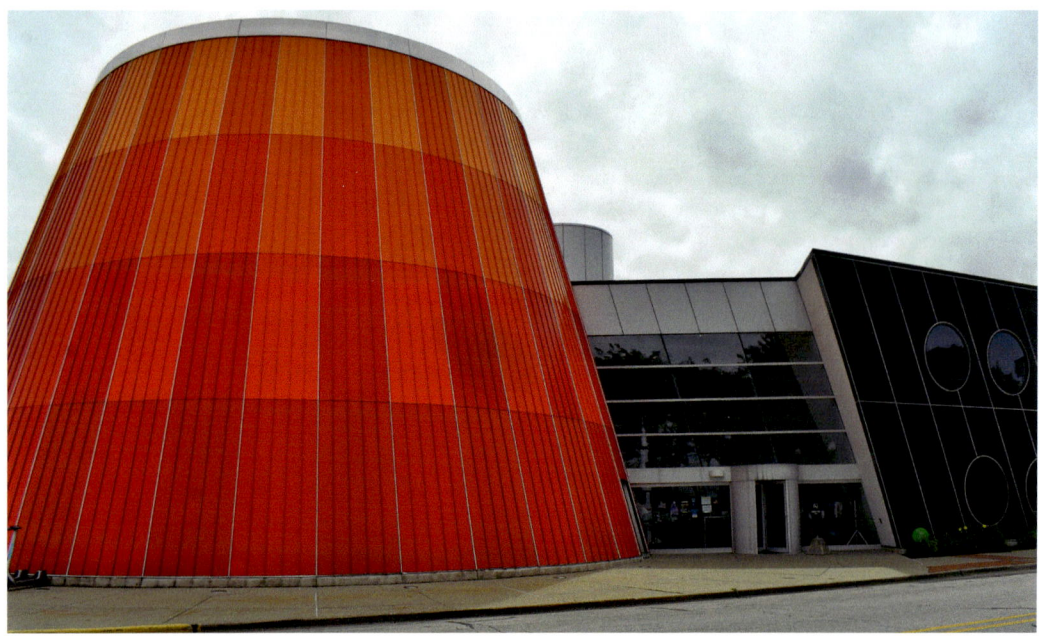

A man and boy snagging a fish on the Saginaw River in Bay City.

The curved, colorful, modern exterior of the Delta College Planetarium in Bay City.

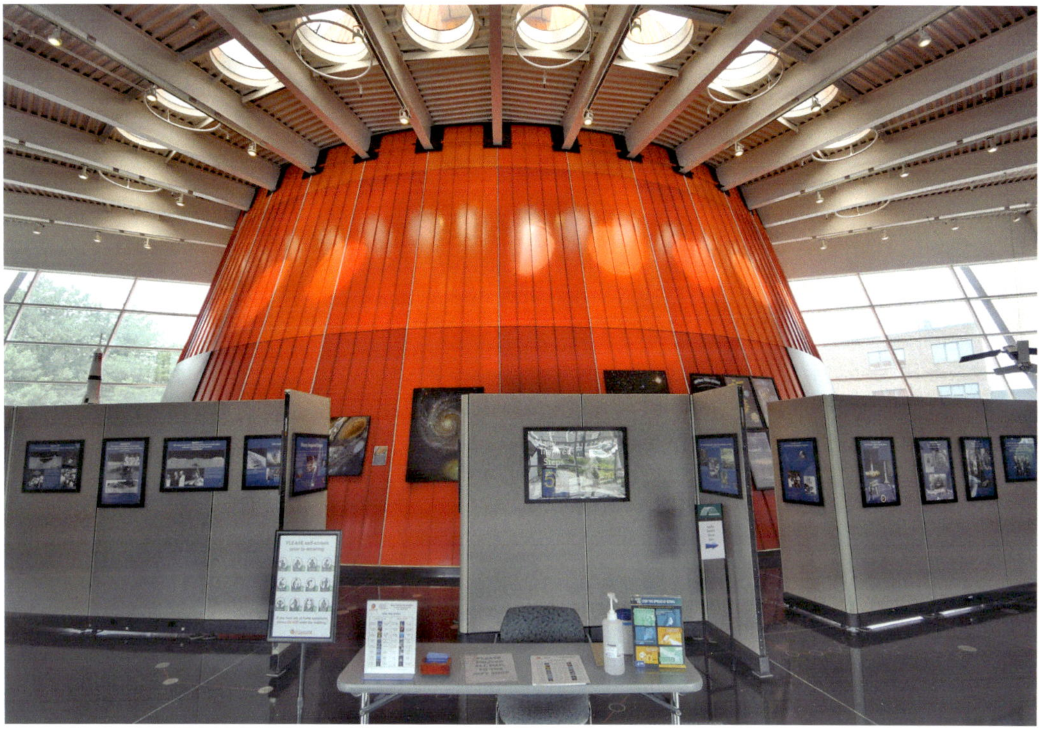

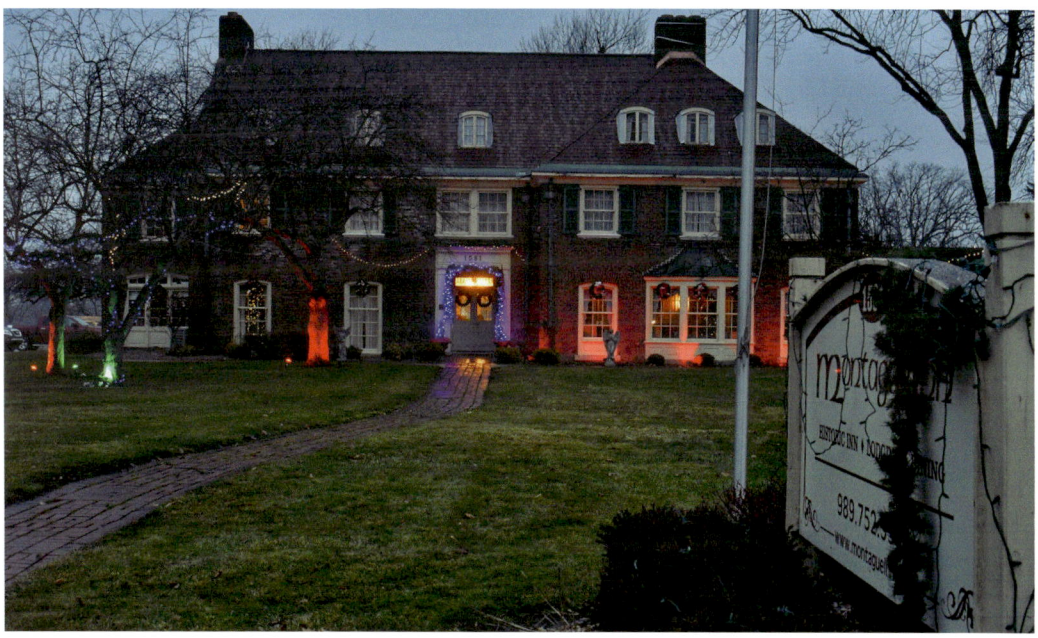

Photographs surround the celestial, circular interior of the Delta College Planetarium in Bay City.

The Montague Inn Bed and Breakfast built in the 1930s in Saginaw glittering with colored lights.

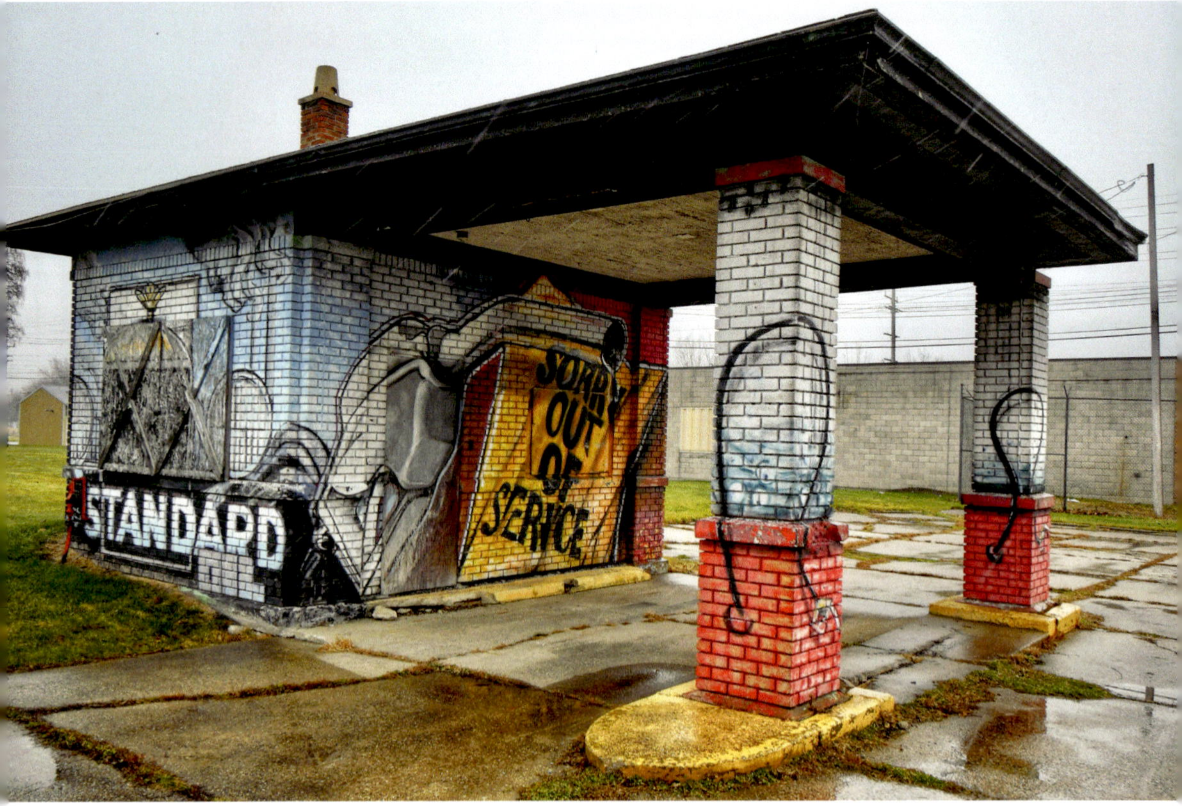

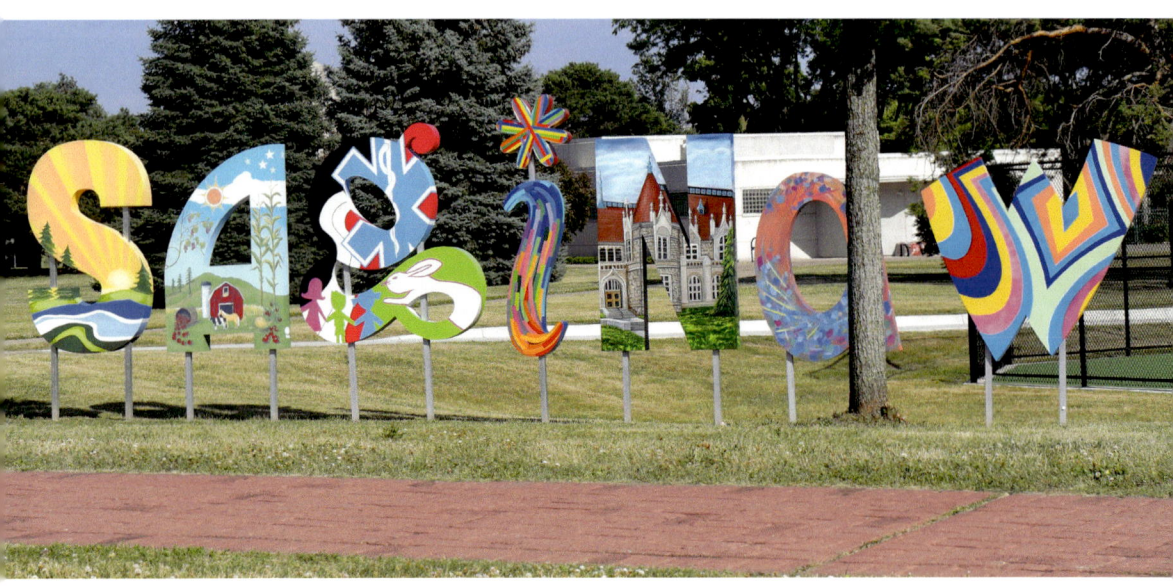

The oldest gas station in Saginaw, Standard Oil, painted with a vibrant mural damp from the rain.

The bold and artistic Saginaw sign welcomes visitors at Celebration Park.

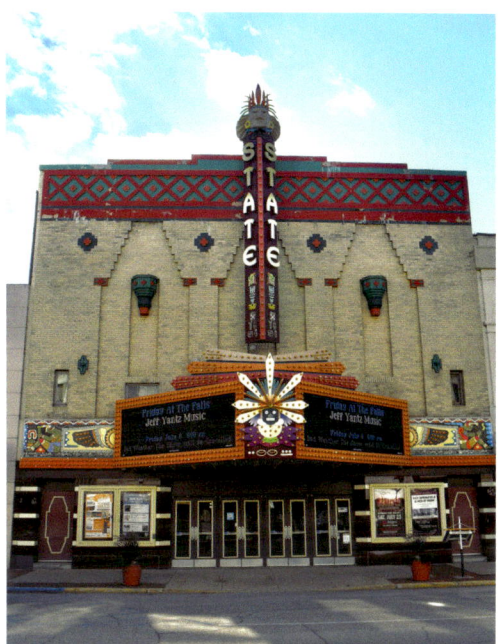

Right: The Mayan-themed State Theater used for burlesque and vaudeville shows in days of yore.

Below: The famed Lee Commons in Saginaw which once housed Rosemary DeGesero, who would walk down the street in her furs with her pet leopard, Chichu.

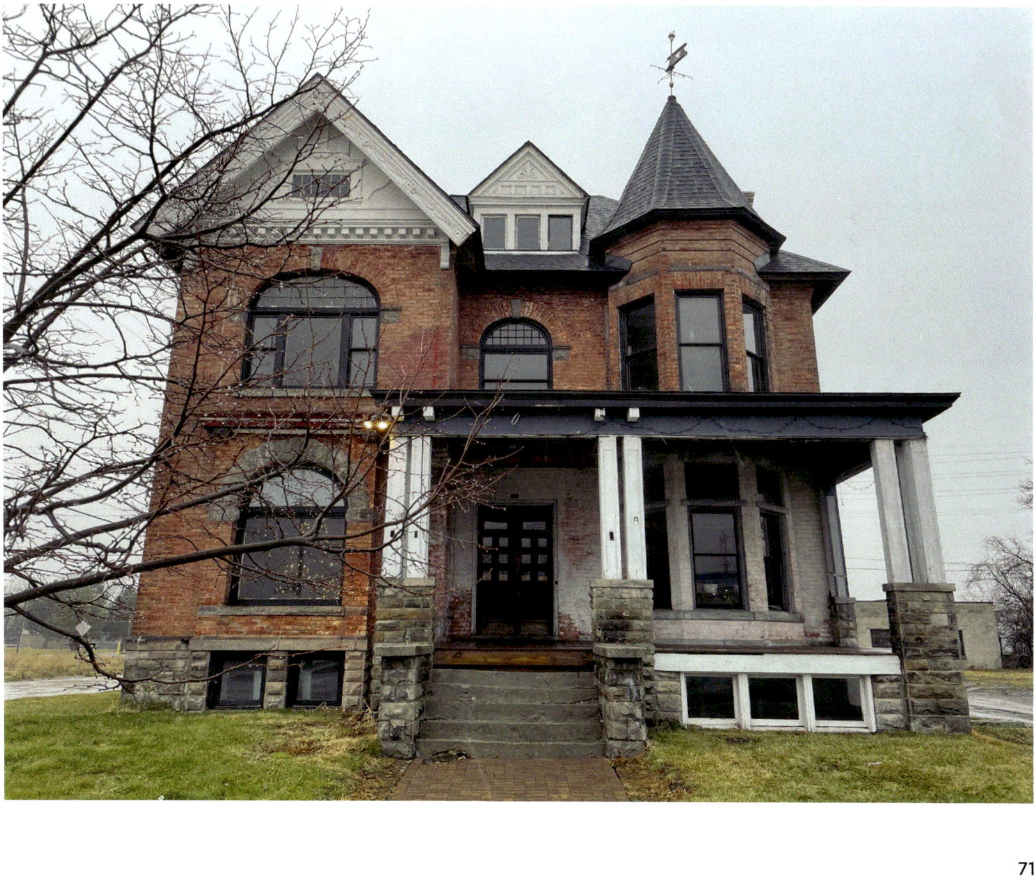

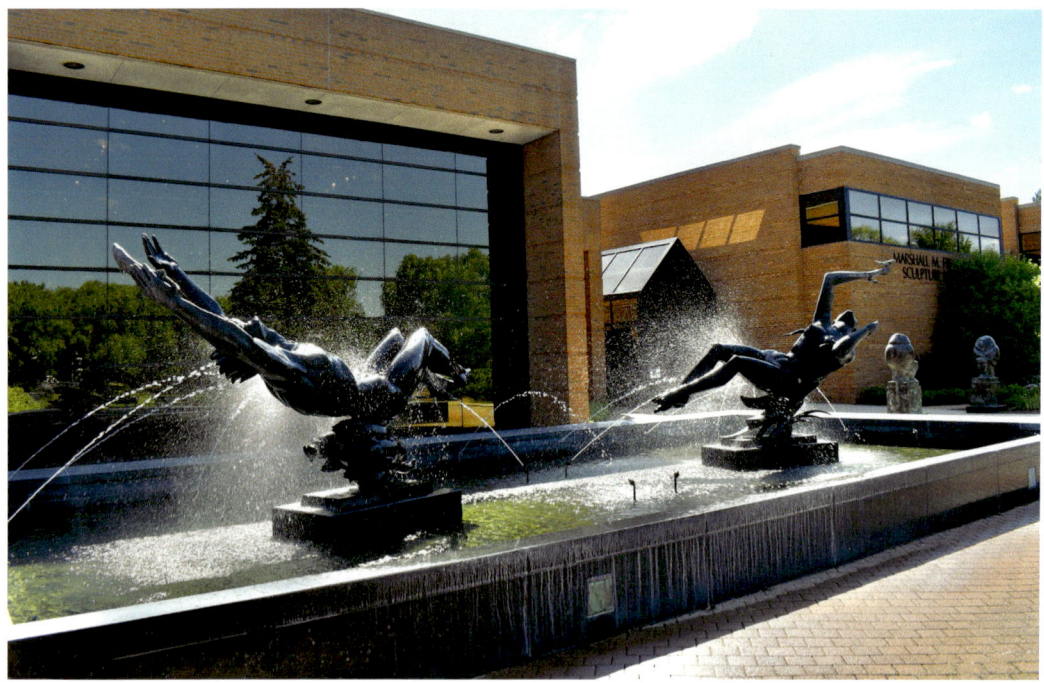

Polished, ebony figures contort and loll in the spray outside the Marshall M. Fredericks Sculpture Museum in Saginaw.

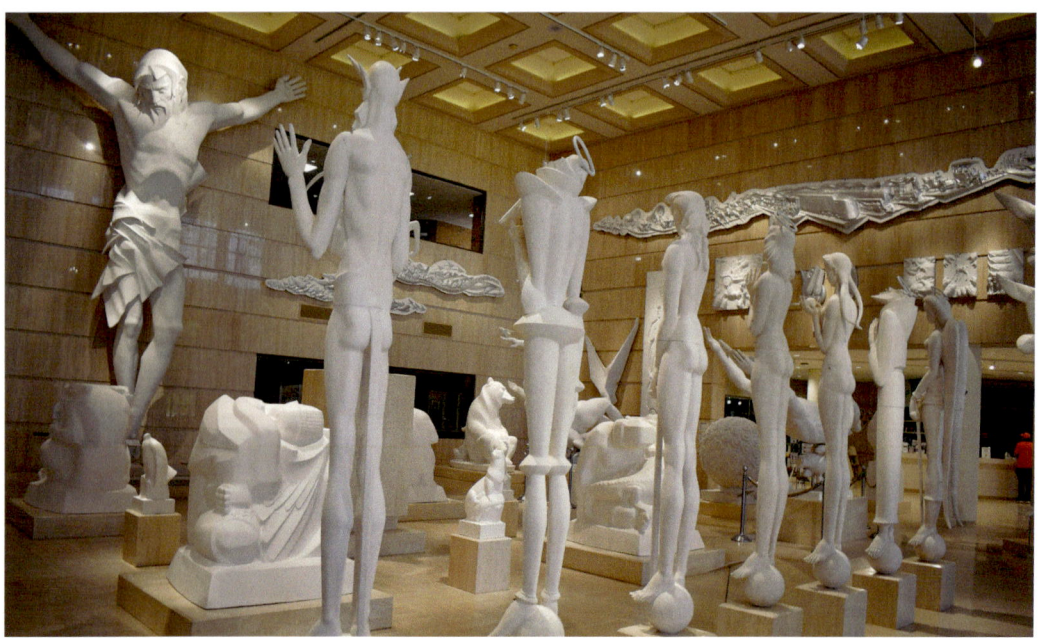

Smooth, white sculptures stand under a blond glow at the Marshall M. Fredericks Sculpture Museum in Saginaw.

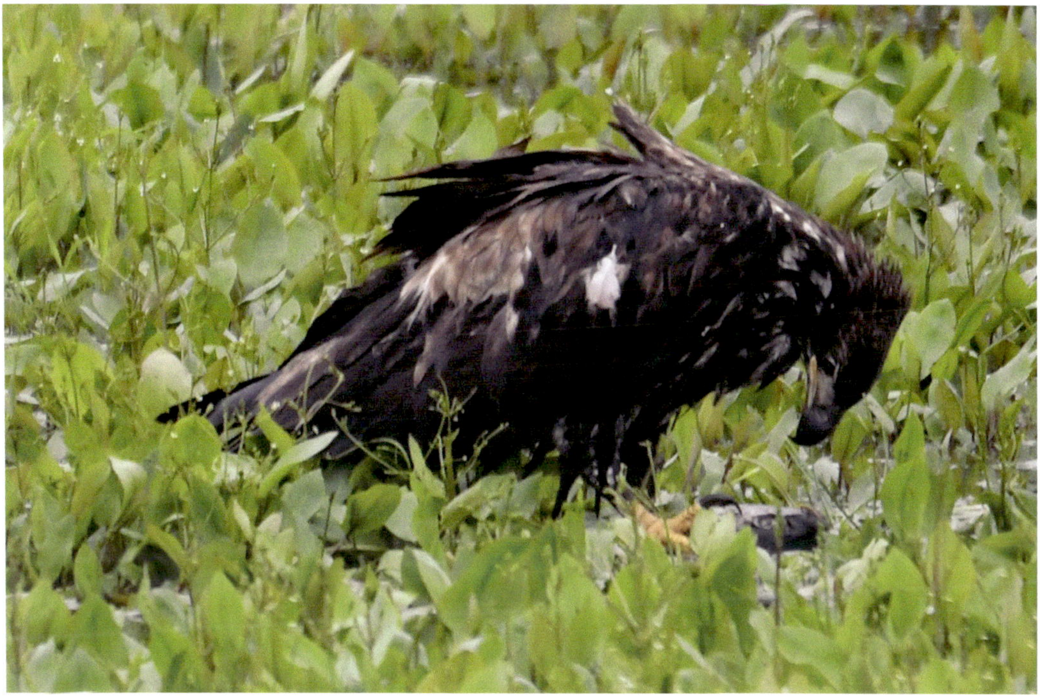

A young bald eagle eats a tasty fish at the Shiawassee National Wildlife Refuge.

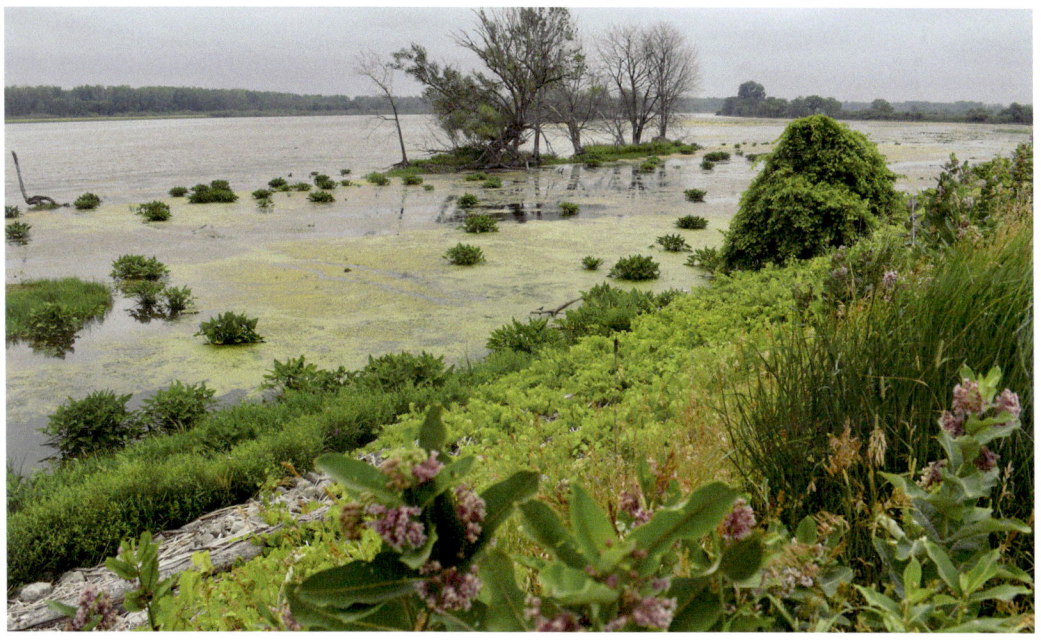

Bottomland forest and rich wetlands filled with a plethora of birds and other wildlife near Saginaw.

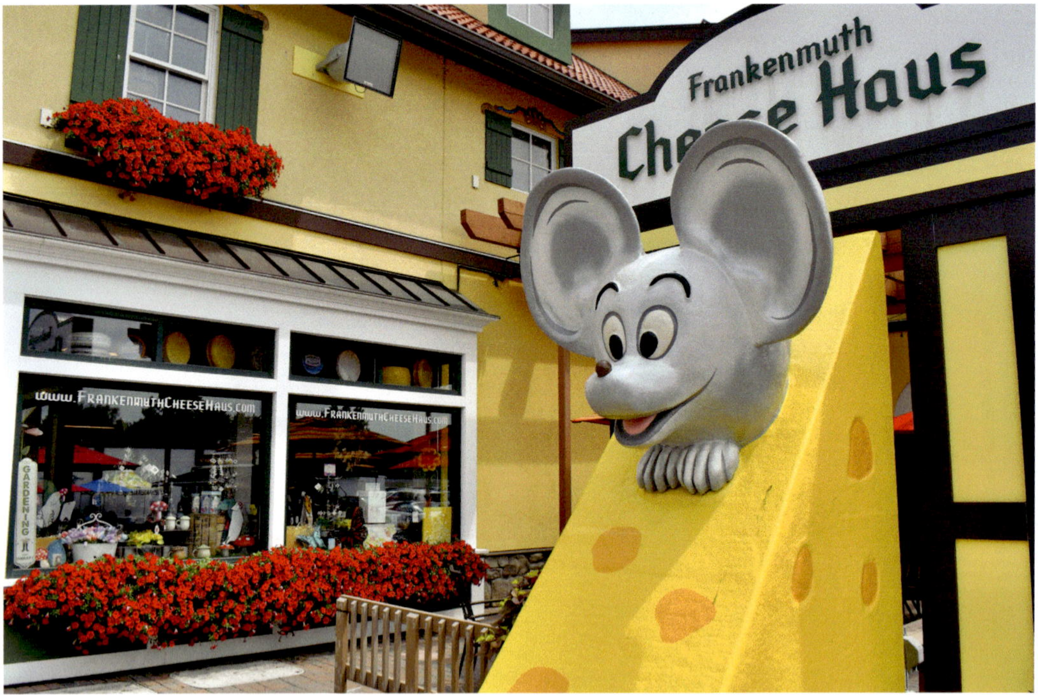

The Frankenmuth Cheese Haus with hundreds of cheeses and its adorable mouse.

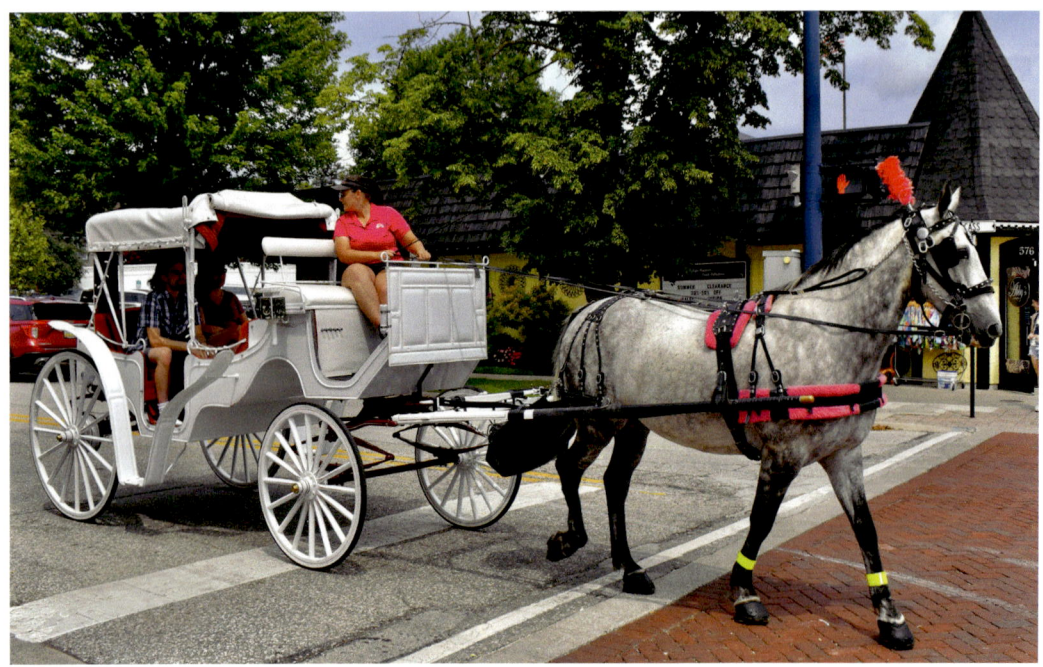

Taking a horse drawn carriage ride in Frankenmuth.

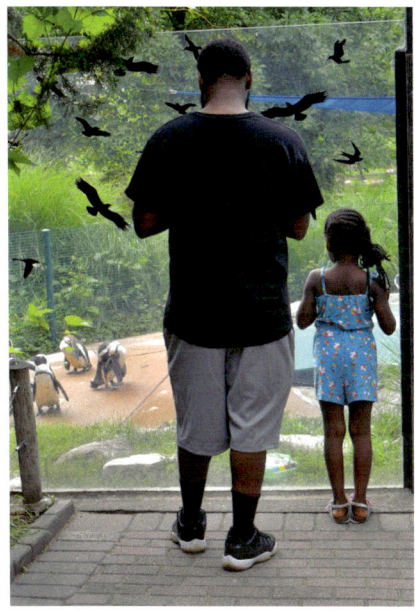

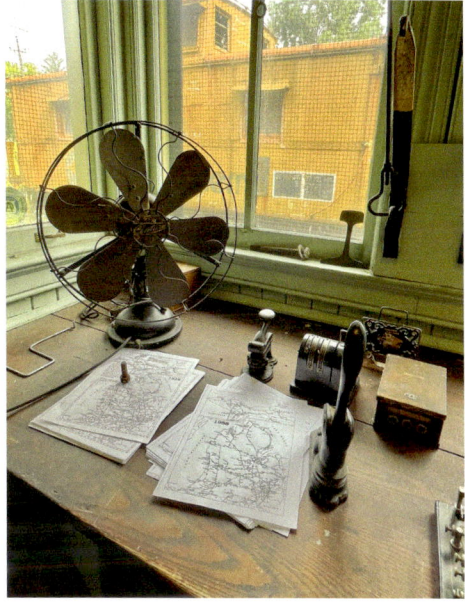

Above left: A father and daughter peering into the penguin exhibit at the Saginaw Children's Zoo.

Above right: Interesting artifacts in an original 1907 Pere Marquette train depot in Saginaw.

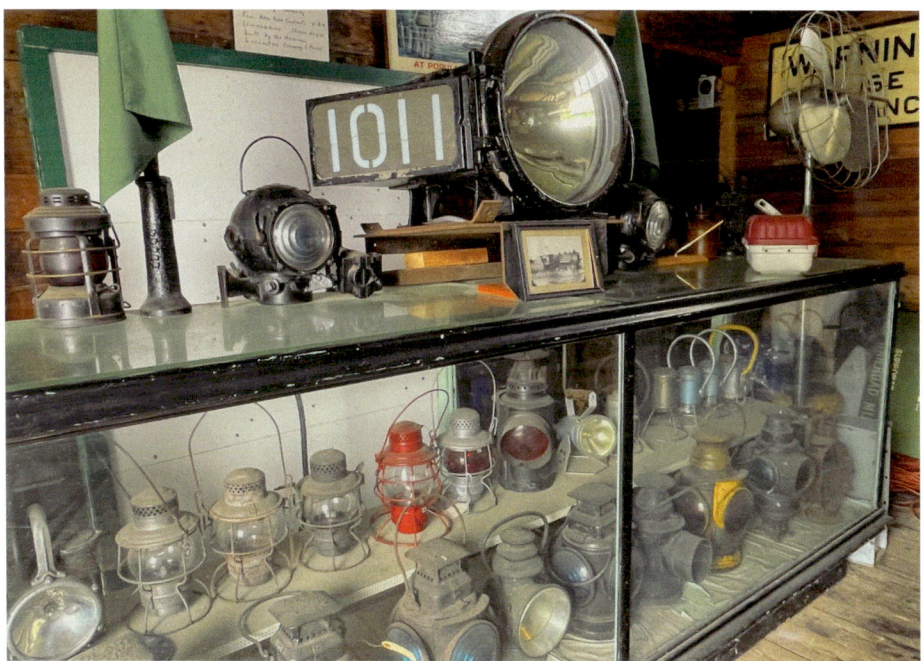

Antique conductor lanterns line the shelves at the Saginaw Railway Museum.

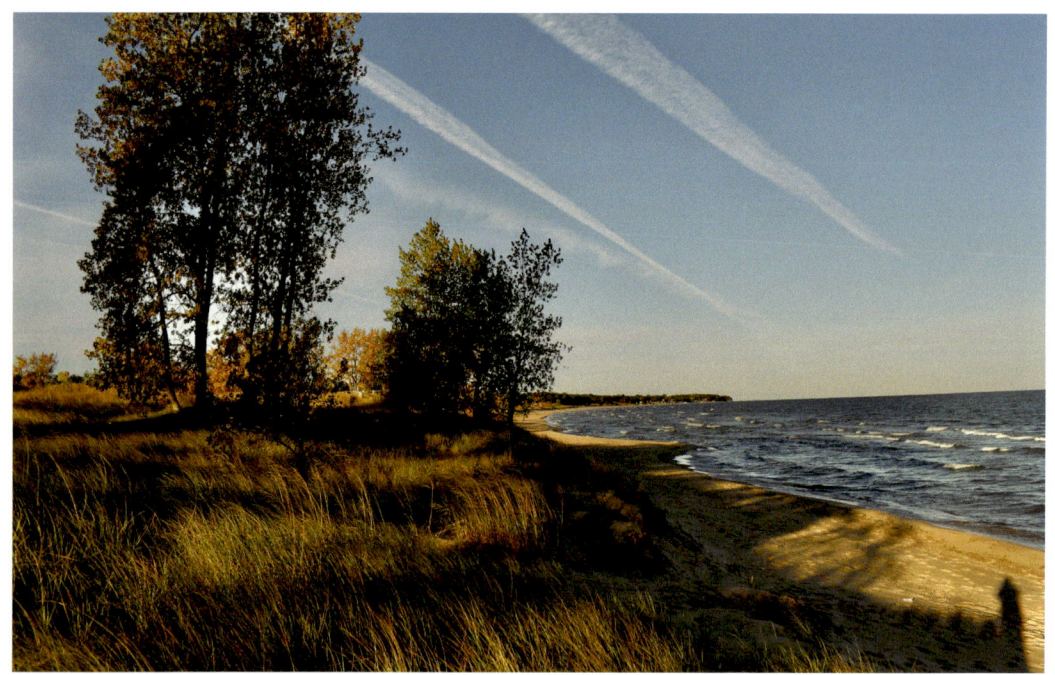

Autumn rays streaking the beach at Port Crescent State Park.

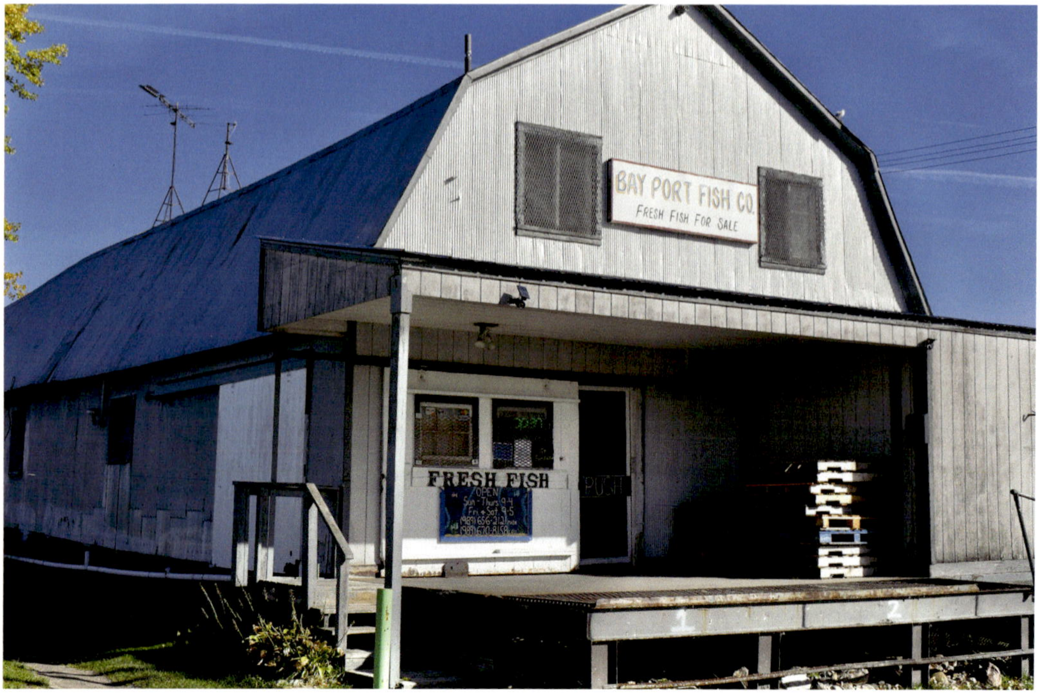

Bay Port Fish Company established in 1895.

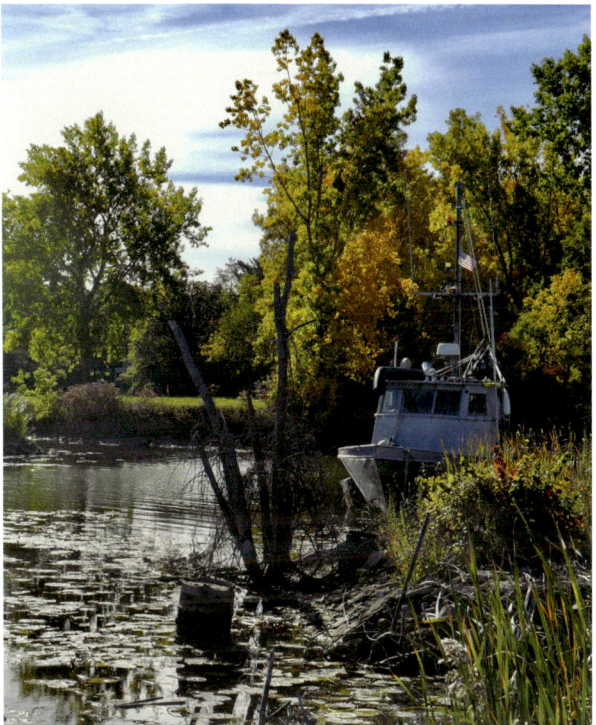

Right: A fishing boat bobs in the sheltered waters after bringing in fresh catch for Bay Port Fish Company.

Below: The Octagon House, once an active place in ages past for social gatherings.

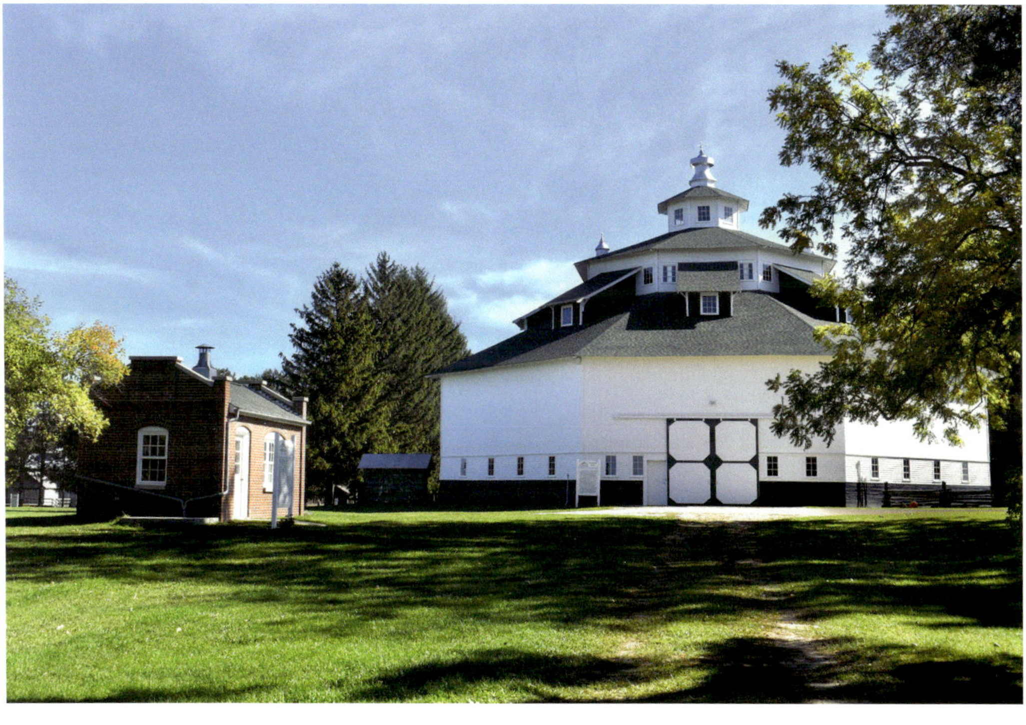

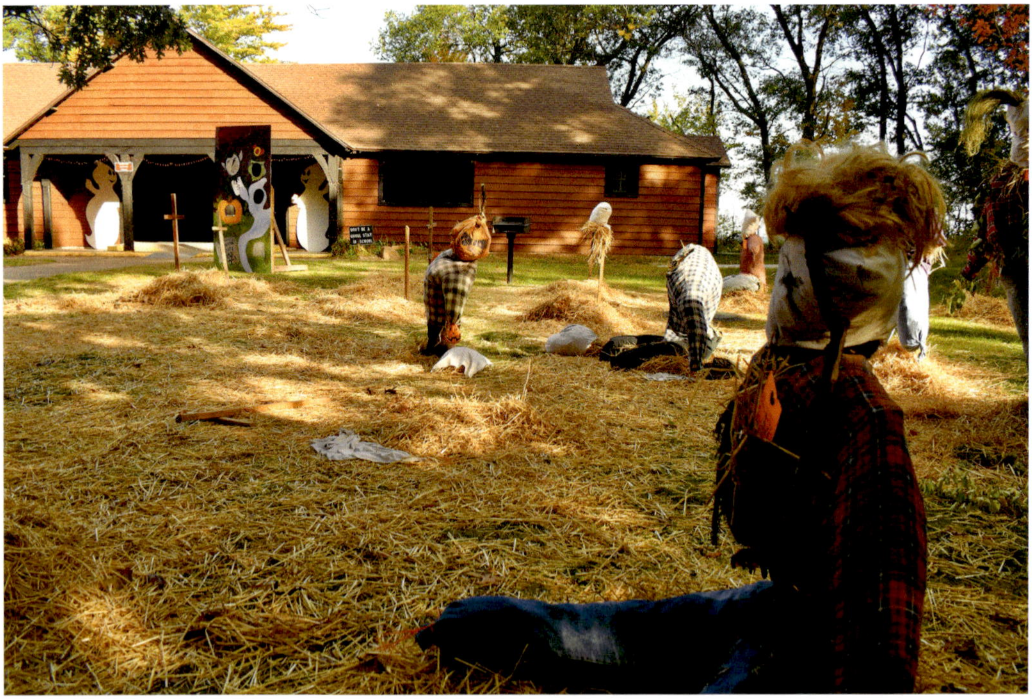

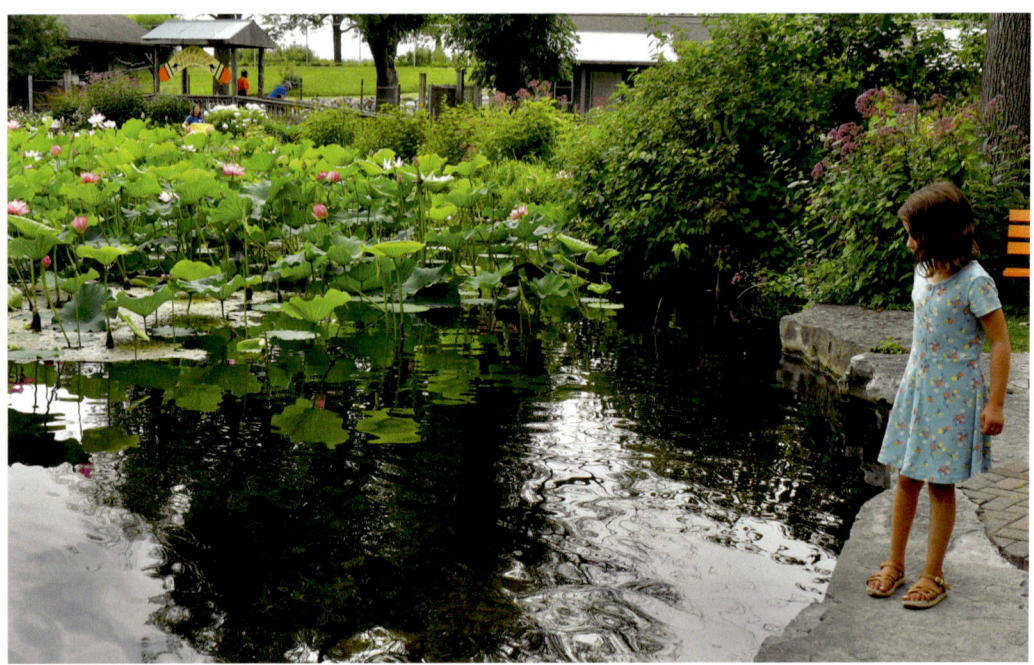

Patchwork scarecrows displayed for a Halloween contest at a Thumb area park.

A young girl staring with fascination into the lily pond at the Saginaw Children's Zoo.

Southwest Region

For-Mar Nature Preserve and Arboretum, at 2141 North Genesee Road, Burton, is celebrating over fifty years of providing wildlife and nature a safe space to thrive. Scattered over 383 scenic acres are lush green woods, brilliant, flowery meadows, and turtle-filled ponds, with hiking paths winding throughout. The arboretum sprawls over 116 of the acres with 1,800 woody plants from 157 species. The arboretum also contains two major gardens: a gorgeous shade garden and rock sculptured geology garden. The visitor's center is a must stop for information about the preserve and to meet live animals that are indigenous to the area. A treehouse, which hosts Nature's Superheroes, The Preservers, begs a visit. Perched 30 feet above the ground, The Preservers' cartoon faces adorn the treehouses inside walls. From this high perch, view the red oak, hickory trees, and basswood that surround the house and the Kearsley creek oxbow trickling below. Another great stop is the Butterfly House to watch the insects drift through the air like brightly painted flowers. Wildlife roams the property, and you may be able to spot deer, muskrats, turtles, frogs, fish, or water bugs skating over the ponds' surface.

Within the historic district of Lapeer is the Pix Theater, at 172 West Nepessing Street. The Pix Theater was built in 1941 and was considered luxurious with its flashing neon marquee and porcelain enamel panels that boasted "the finest of entertainment." The theater sported a state-of-the-art cooling system where icy well water was dumped in coils to chill the air. Today, the theater still retains its vintage art deco facade and retro marquee. Buy a ticket to enjoy a movie from the past on its vintage one screen.

Nestled next to the Pix Theater is Gallery 194, at 194 W. Nepessing Street, Lapeer. The gallery hosts local area artists in its shows and offers classes if you want to satisfy your creative side. Walk the gallery and view its lovely works.

In 1819, a fur trader Jacob Smith founded the village of Flint. Flint, along with Saginaw and Bay City, had explosive growth during the late 1800s due to the lumber industry's growth. Saginaw Street, Flint's main street, is still paved with bricks and has been since the lumber boom. Flint later became the leading manufacturer of carriages followed by the automobile, earning the city the title of "Vehicle City." General Motors was created in Flint in 1908 and made the town a manufacturing powerhouse. Today, there remains the General Motors Flint Assembly Plant built in 1947 after World War II, which now produces full-size pickup trucks.

Applewood Estate, also known as the Charles Stewart Mott House, at 1400 East Kearsley Street, Flint, is an enchanting 34-acre property in the center of the city. The house and the buildings were constructed by automotive pioneer Charles Stewart Mott. The grounds were named for the apple orchard and in memory of Charles' father, who once owned Mott's Inc., notable for their applesauce. Drift through the sculpted gardens exploding with heavenly perennials. Stop at Demonstration Garden with its gurgling fountain, polished statue, and savory herbs, designed to stimulate inspiration in the viewer. Head to the mansion and explore on tour the furnishings once used by the family, such as the sixteenth-century Italian carved wooden chest and the 1800 solid mahogany table with brass paws used for dining. The attractive property and home provide a welcome respite from the city and a wonderful way to experience a past era.

After taking in city, head to Italia Gardens on 3273 Miller Road, Flint, to enjoy some homemade pasta goodness. Established in 1931, the establishment was the first Italian restaurant in the city. Today it is still serving up such traditional fare as a hearty lasagna, succulent chicken piccata, and a dish created by its founder, spitini, pan-fried sliced steak served on a skewer with onion and bay leaf.

An eclectic store seeped in history is Paul's Pipe Shop at 647 Saginaw Street, Flint. Founded in 1928, the fifteen-year-old Paul T. Spaniola started the business after a $10 bet, saying he couldn't get anyone to buy a pipe. He ran it until he was almost 100 years old, then his son, Dan, took the business over and still runs it today at seventy years old. The business houses a museum with over 2,000 pipes, antique cigarette boxes, and vintage smoking paraphernalia. The wall is decorated with awards and images, including one of the late actress Susan Hayward who needed to be taught how to smoke a pipe by Paul Spaniola for her 1953 film, *The President's Lady*. Fewer people are smoking today because of the surgeon general's warning, but the shop is still a piece of eclectic Flint history.

With its vivid patchwork brick and glass exterior, the Flint Institute of Arts Museum at 1120 East Kearsley Street, Flint, is the second largest art museum in Michigan. The bright white rooms are hung with European and American works fifteenth century to the present in a collection of over 8,000 pieces. The museum hosts numerous events, such as Coffee with the Curator, and exhibits, which have included artists such as Picasso and Rodin. It is a great place to relax and get your art on.

Across the street from the Flint Art Museum is the Sloan Museum of Discovery and Longway Planetarium at 1221 East Kearsley Street, Flint. The Sloan Museum exhibits feature historic automobiles, regional history, and plenty of hands-on science for the kids. View hundreds of artifacts from Flint's boisterous twentieth-century history, then walk to Discovery Hall to interact with the Great Lakes water table. When your feet begin to ache, slip into one of the comfy seats at the Longway Planetarium and watch a movie glowing all around you.

Journey back to the late 1800s at Crossroads Village and Huckleberry Railroad at 6140 North Bray Road, Flint. Walk down the avenue of a living history museum with its thirty-four historic buildings, including an operating grist mill, a vintage barber shop, a general store, and a blacksmith shop. Watch artisans plying their craft then head to the Colwell Opera House to view a show. Finish off with an enjoyable ride on the Huckleberry Railroad, pulled by the authentic diesel Engine #12 or the coal-burning Engine #152. The village is an awesome place to get your steps in while enjoying local history.

Capitol Theater, at 140 East 2nd Street, Flint, with its towering neon sign and beautifully restored facade, has had a presence in the city since 1928. Enter the lobby with its golden bloom vaulted ceiling that shimmers above. The auditorium greets eyes with a deep sapphire sky dotted with sparkling stars that wink at the ten brilliant peacocks perched above the stage, guarded by faux-marble columns. The architecture transports the viewer to a Mediterranean patio in the midst of a garden. Catch a performing art show or just visit to enjoy the theater's picturesque ambiance.

Rising above the town with its glittering white Doric columns and gable front, the Greek Revival historic Lapeer Courthouse, at 235 West Nepessing Street, Lapeer, is the oldest working courthouse in Michigan. The courthouse was built in 1845 by one of the Lapeer's first settlers, Alvin N. Hart. The building has all its original features including a three-tiered tower that looms in the back. Inside are polished hardwood benches and trim. A grassy square with benches surrounds the courthouse, providing an ideal spot for a brief rest. The building is available for rental for receptions and special events.

Piety Hill Historic District, located in the downtown of Lapeer and encompassing twenty-eight buildings, is a wonderful place to take a leisurely ramble. The district is bordered by North Main Street, Park Street, and West Nepessing Street. Added to the National Register of Historic Places in 1985, the assortment of structures was built from 1830–1950 and includes a tavern, a library, a school, five churches, an engine house, and houses in various styles, from striking Greek Revival to ornate Queen Anne. Eagle Tavern, located at 237 N. Main Street, is one of the most significant. Used as a tavern at a stagecoach stop until 1850, the bar has since been converted to a family residence and was part of the Underground Railroad.

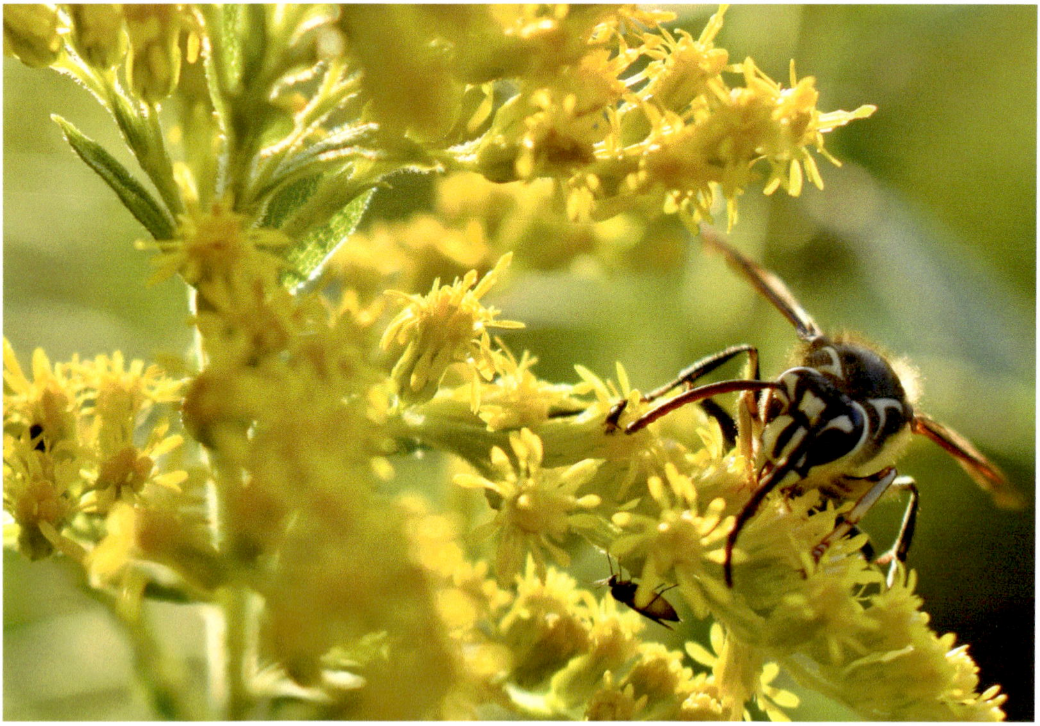

An insect drinks the sweet nectar from a wildflower in a flaxen meadow in Peck.

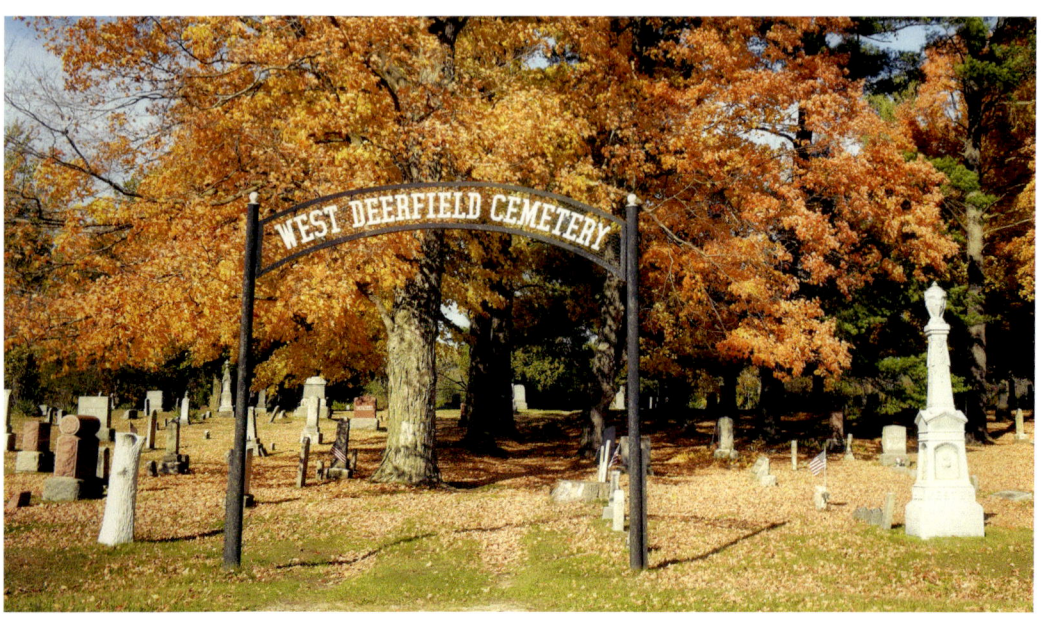

West Deerfield Cemetery, one of the many little graveyards tucked amongst the trees and fields, housing the ancestors of the small towns' inhabitants.

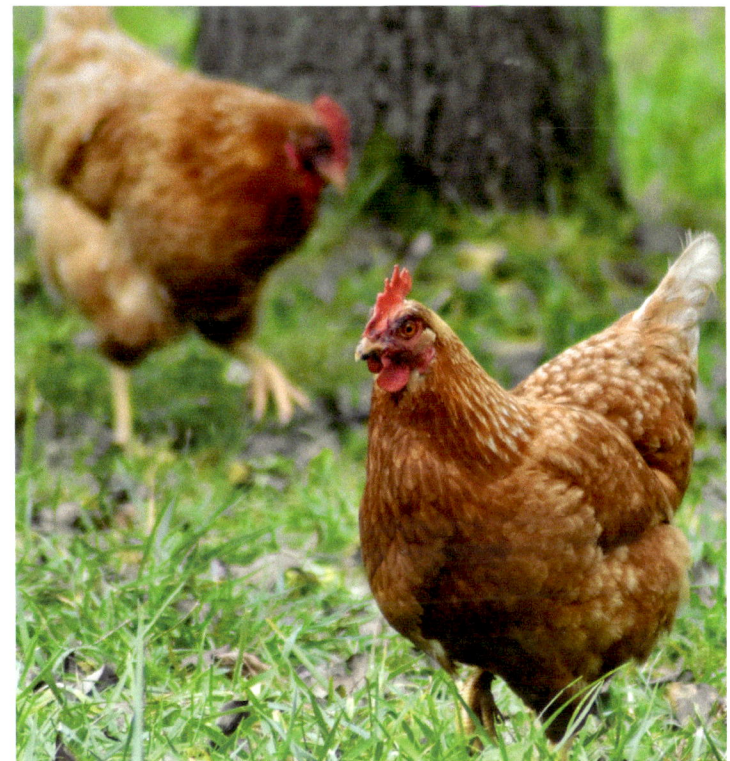

Right: Clucking hens searching for tasty bugs in the meadow.

Below: The Flint River reflecting a lemon dawn.

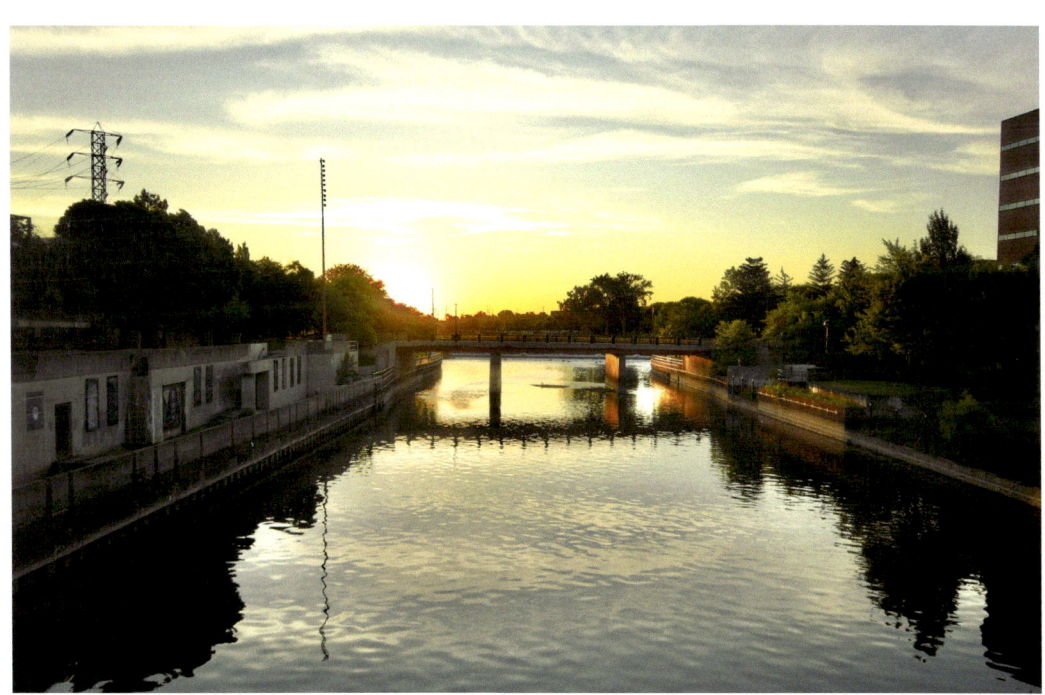

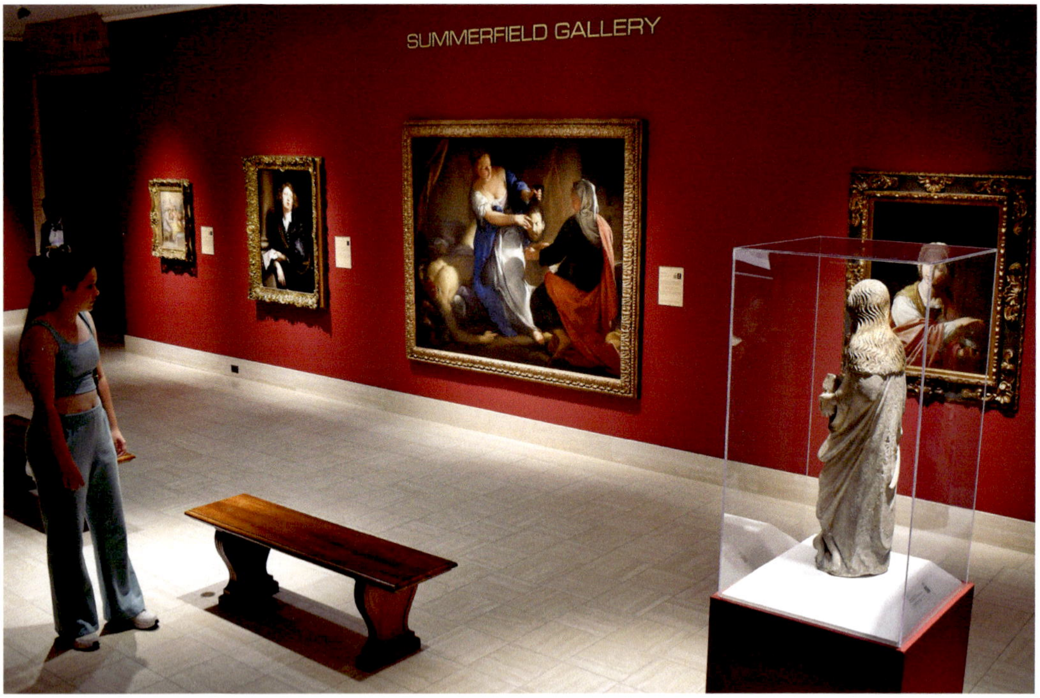

SUMMERFIELD GALLERY

A woman appreciating a breathtaking sculpture at the Flint Institute of Arts.

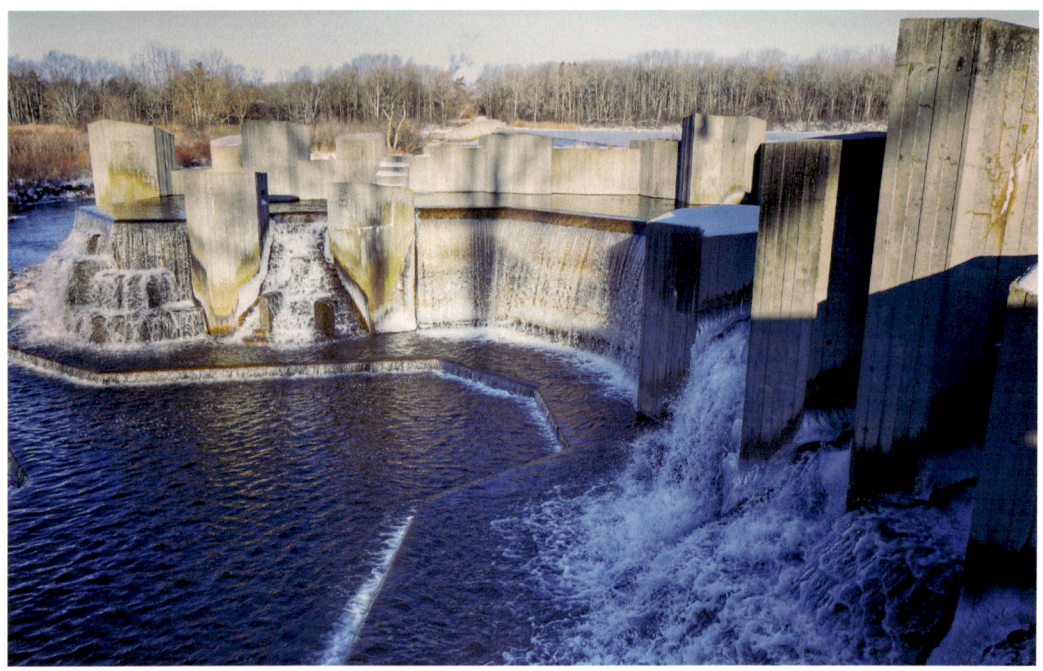

Stepping Stone Falls bubbling in the crisp winter air.

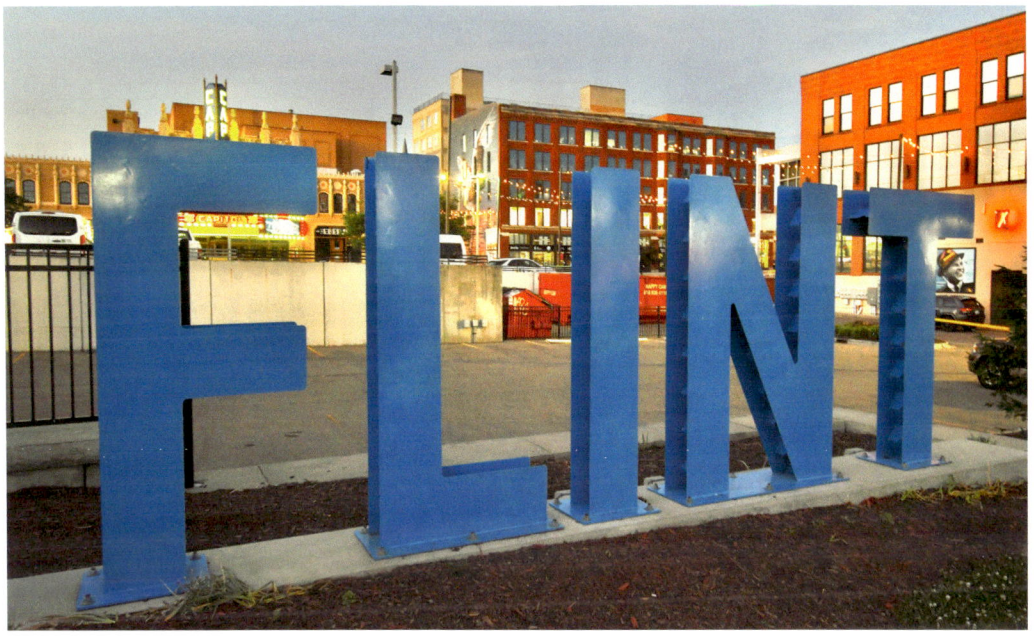

The city of Flint welcomes visitors with its stately sapphire blue sign.

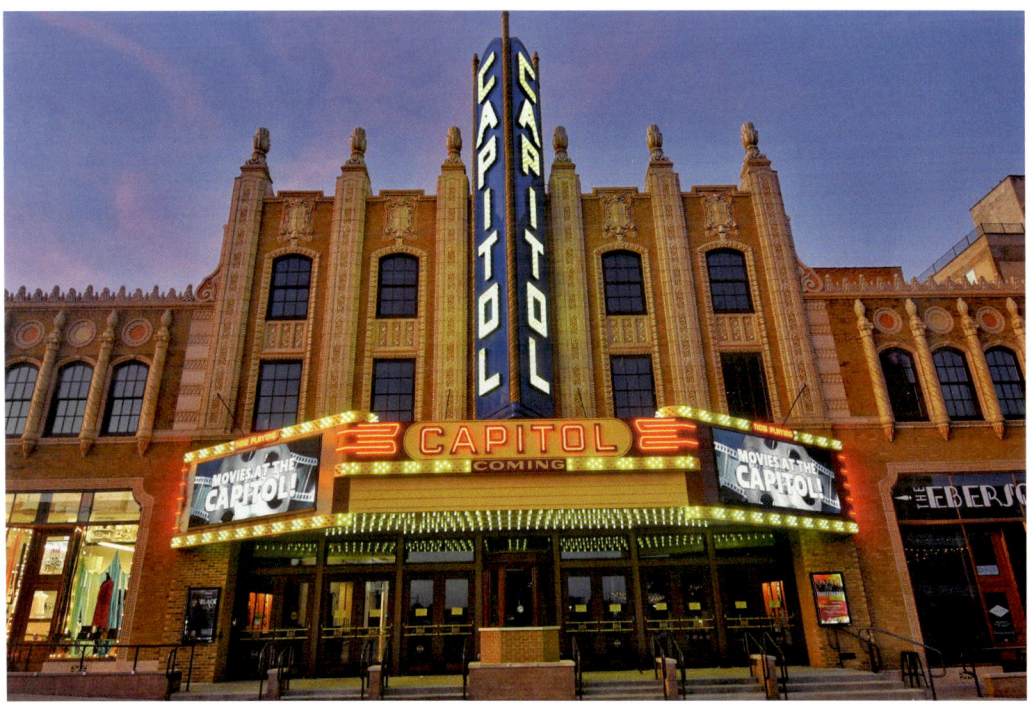

The retro Capitol Theater in Flint with its historic facade highlighted with the marquee's luminous lights.

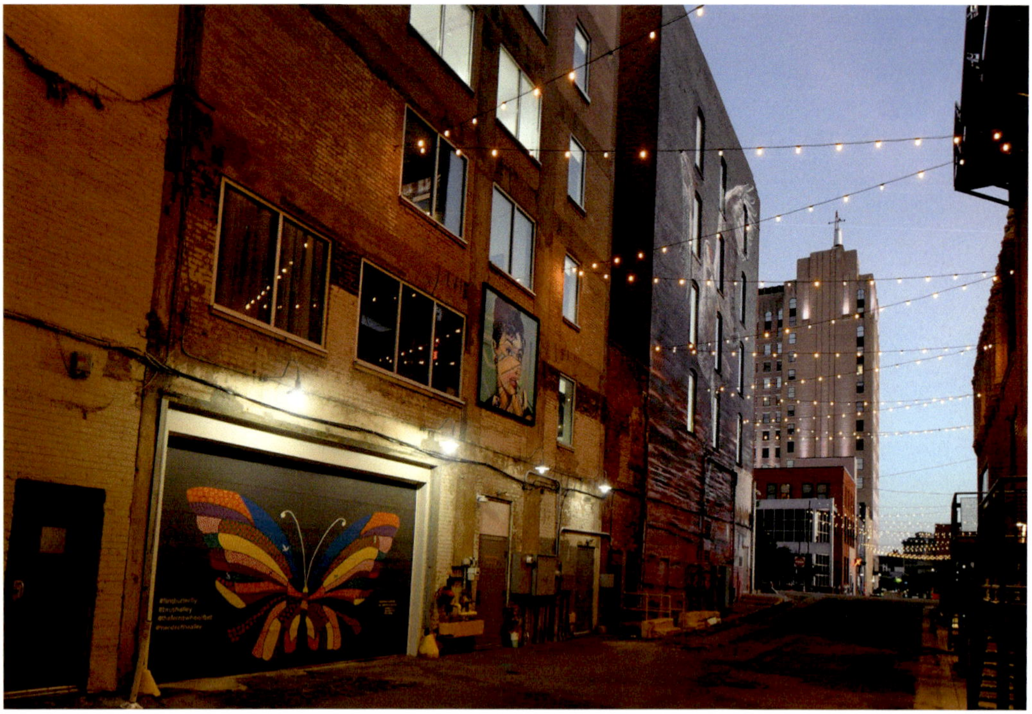

A sparkling alley in Flint where artists painted vivid murals.

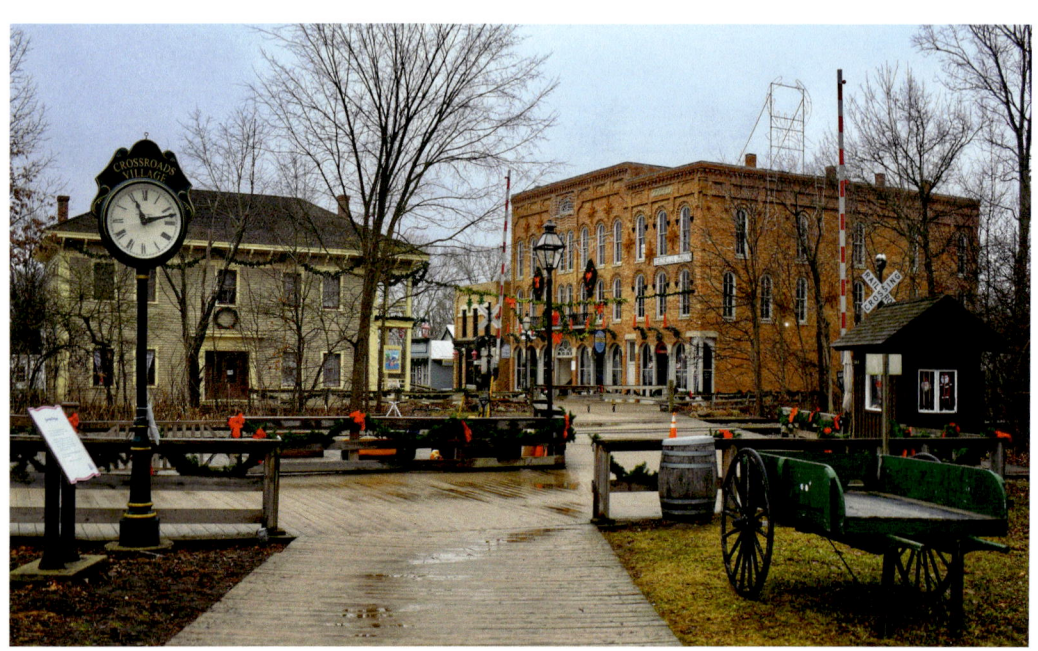

Crossroads Village in Flint decorated for the festive holidays.

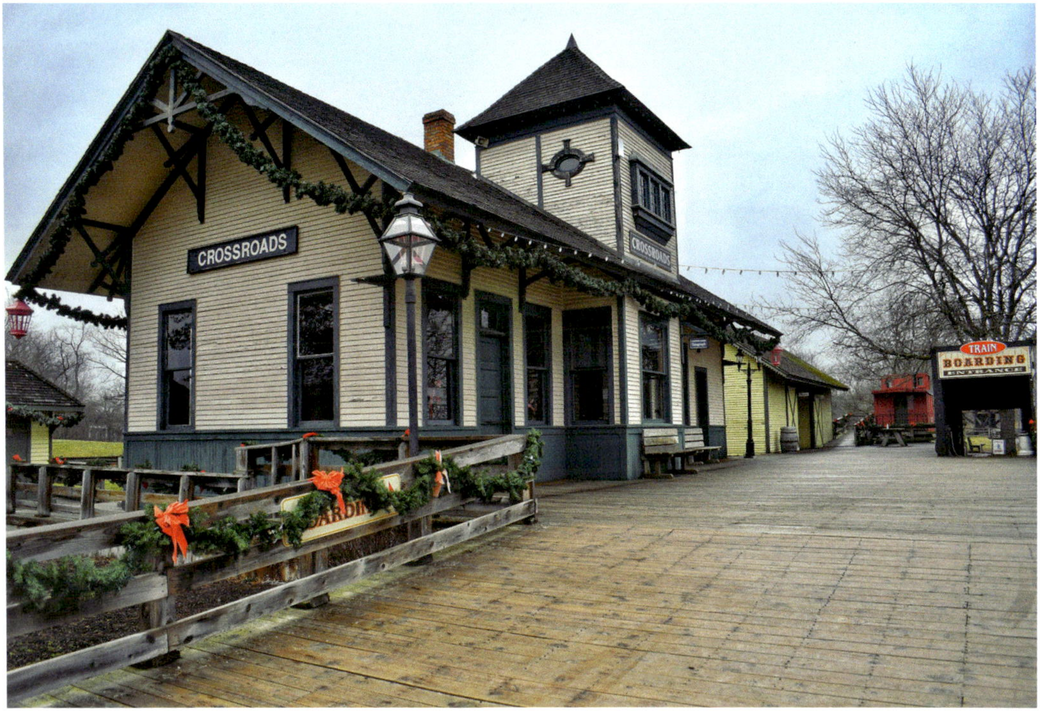

Above: Huckleberry Railroad station festooned with piney garlands for Christmas.

Right: A snow-iced ebony mustang standing in a flake-covered field.

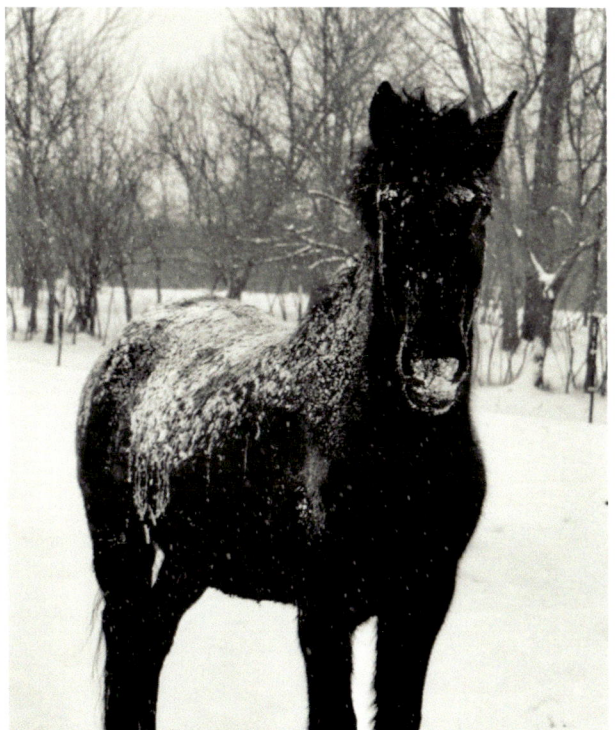

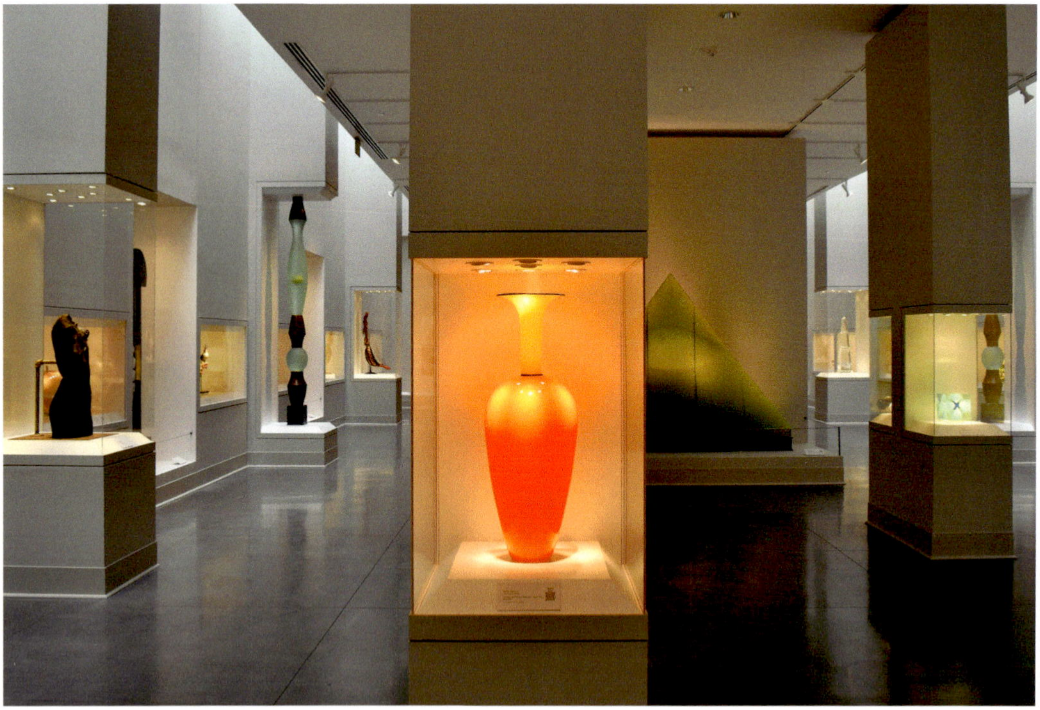

Above: Shimmering glass glowing in its cases at the Flint Institute of Arts.

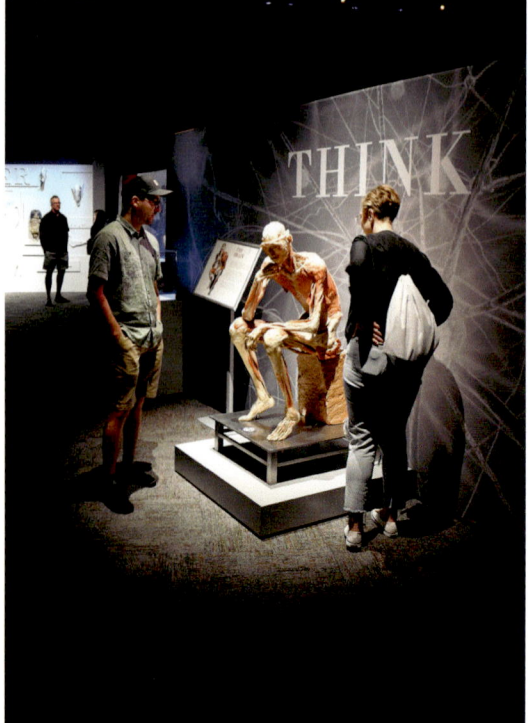

Left: The intriguing Think display at the Human Exhibit in the Sloan Museum in Flint.

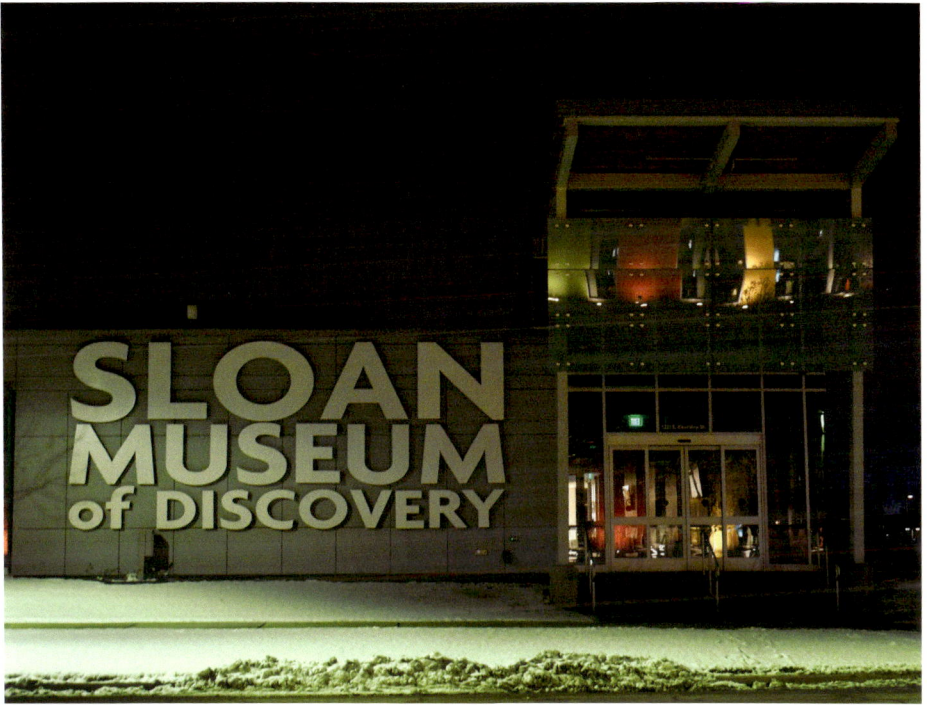

The entrance to the Sloan Museum swathed in an emerald cast.

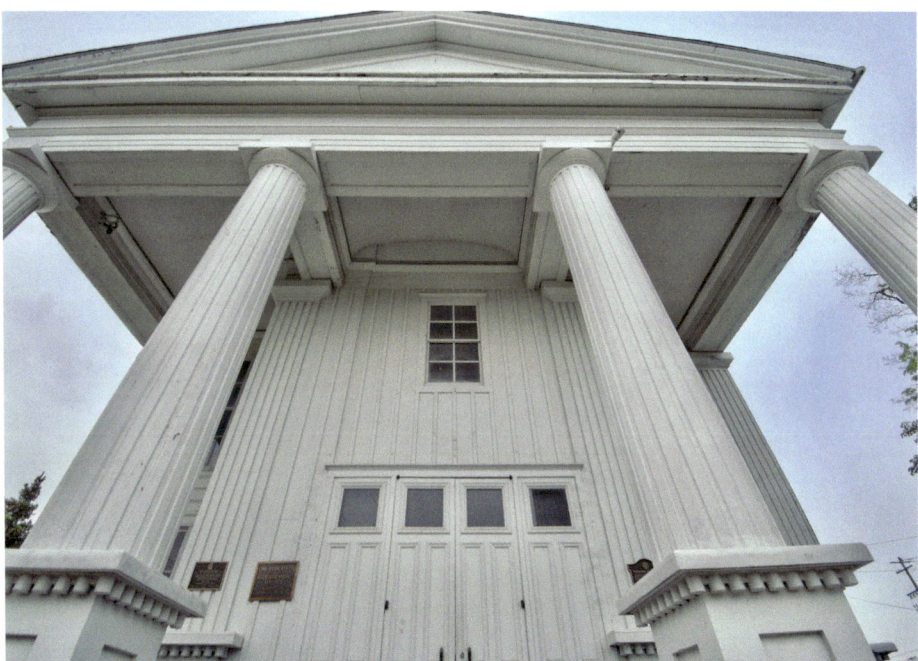

The historic Greek Revival courthouse in Lapeer, rising boldly to the sky, built in 1845.

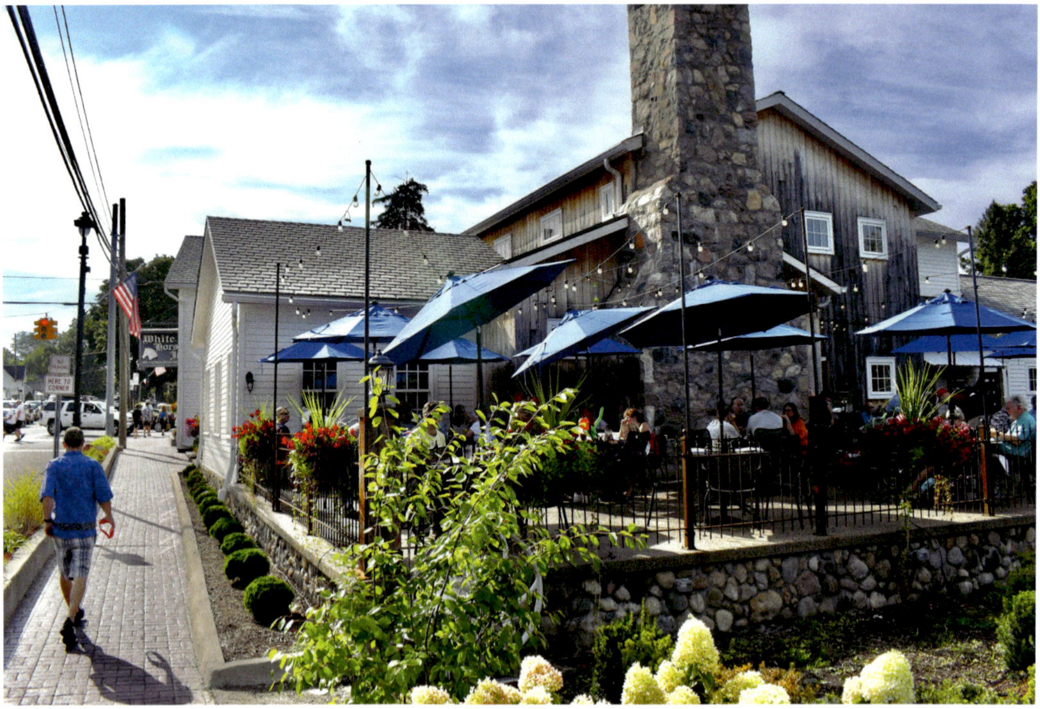

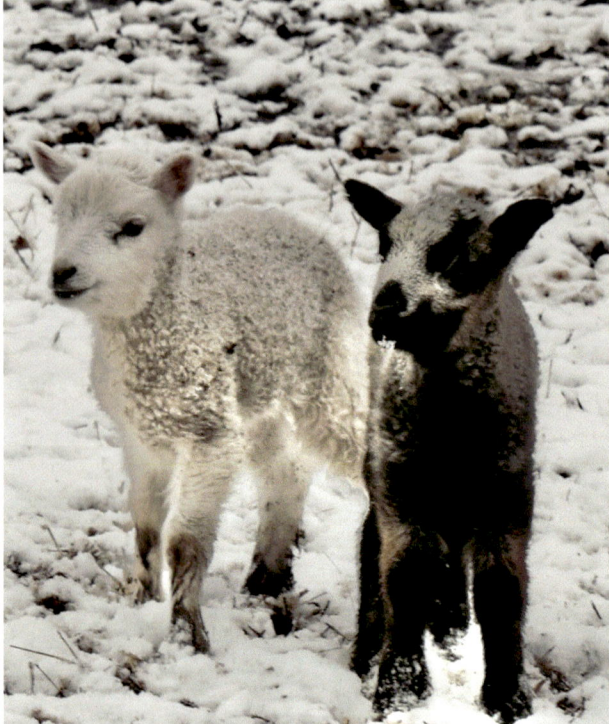

Above: The White Horse Inn in Metamora, built in the 1850s, with an outdoor patio to enjoy a summer day.

Left: Woolly, baby lambs born on snowy spring afternoon.

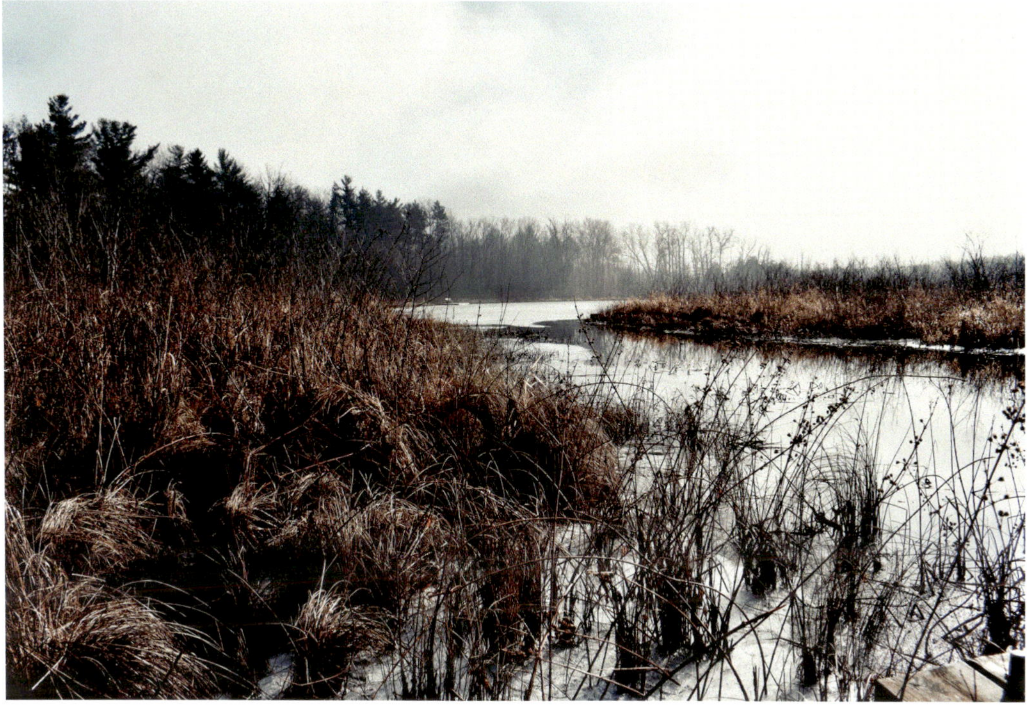

Above: The stark, crystal-scattered landscape at Seven Ponds Nature Center on a sharp, winter afternoon.

Right: The celebrated mansion with its spraying fountain at Applewood Estate in Flint.

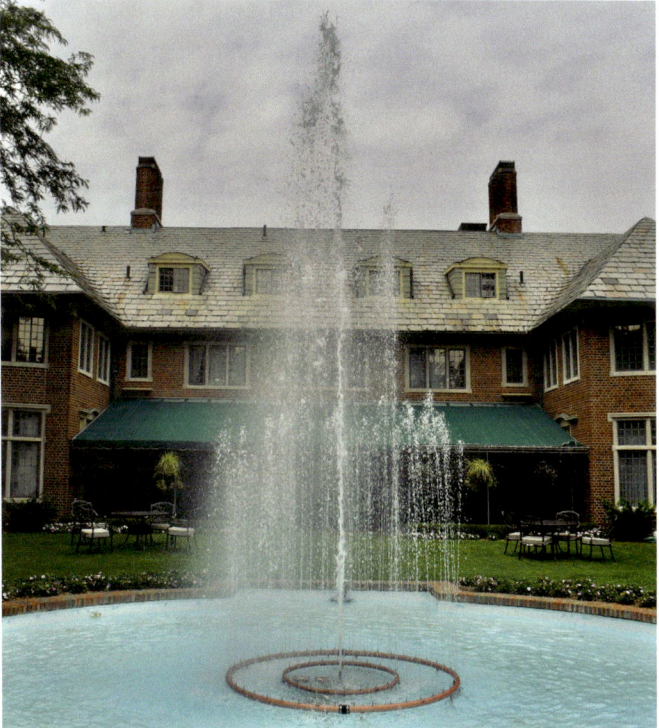

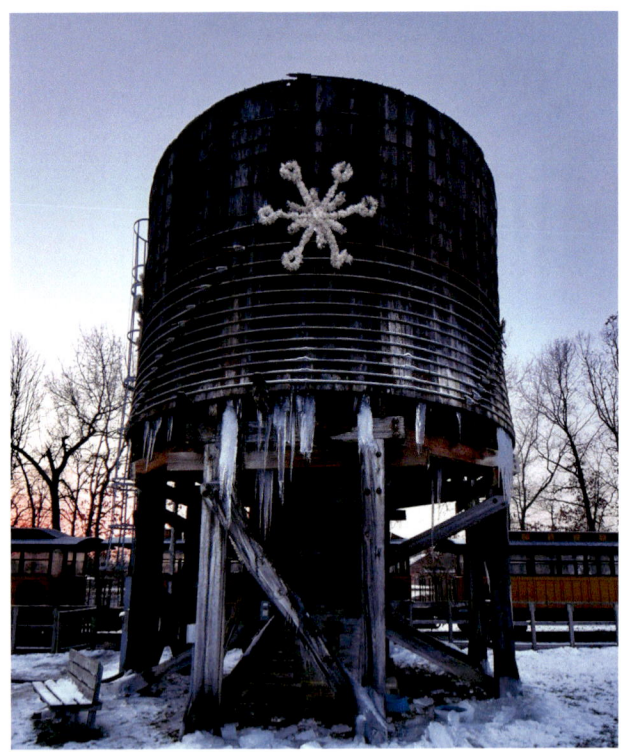

Left: The antique water tower, costumed in icicles, at Crossroads Village in Flint.

Below: The tree house, roosting quietly, at For-Mar Nature Preserve and Arboretum in Burton.

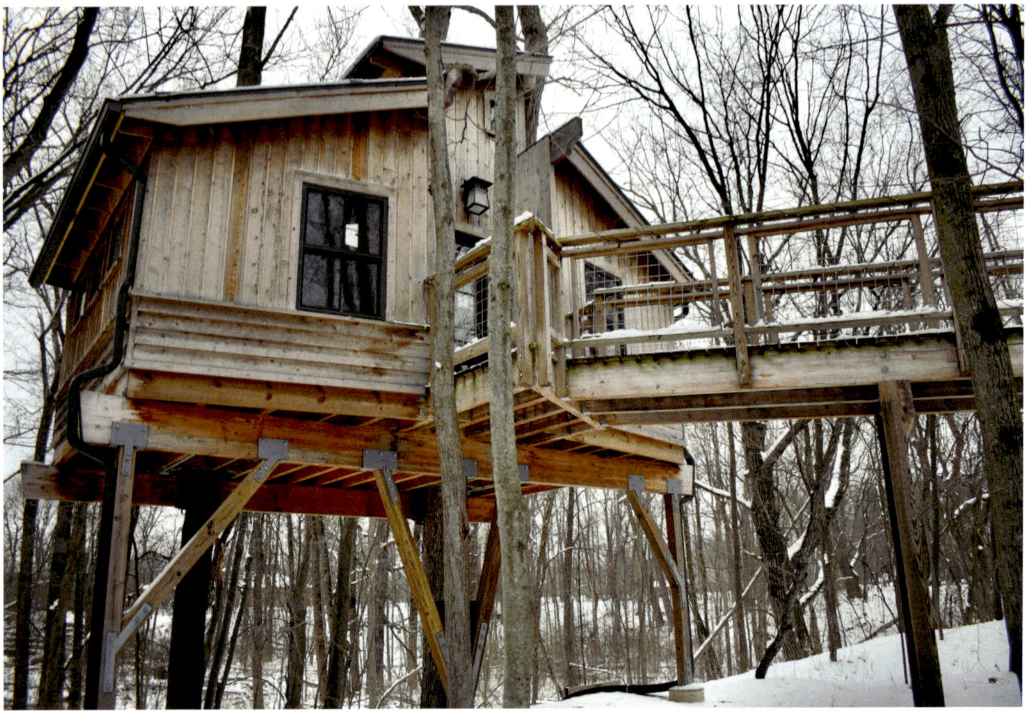

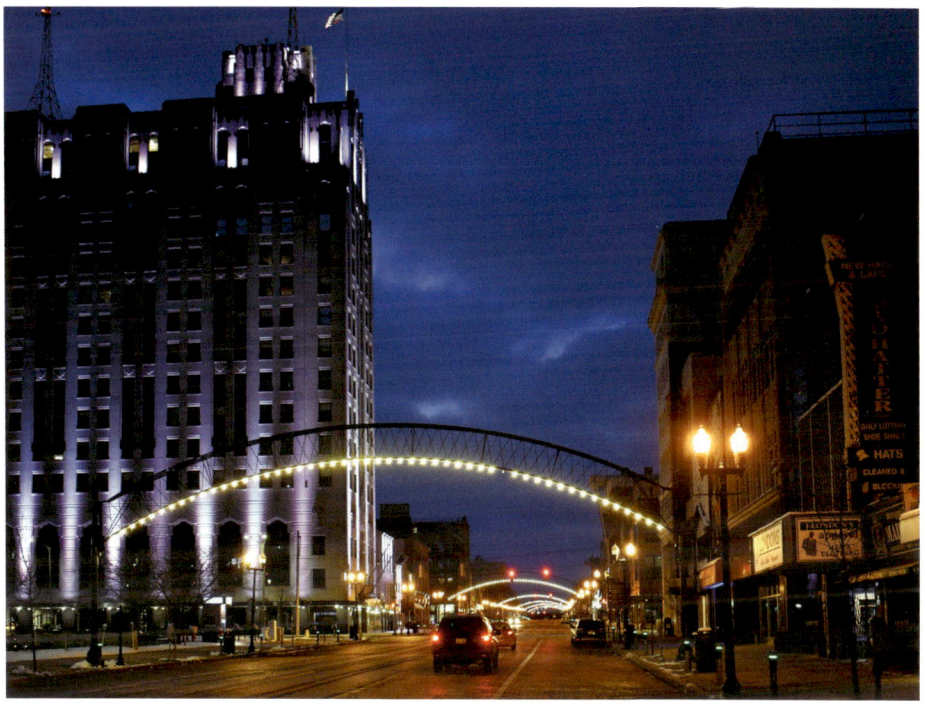

Downtown Flint bathed in a warm radiance on Saginaw Street.

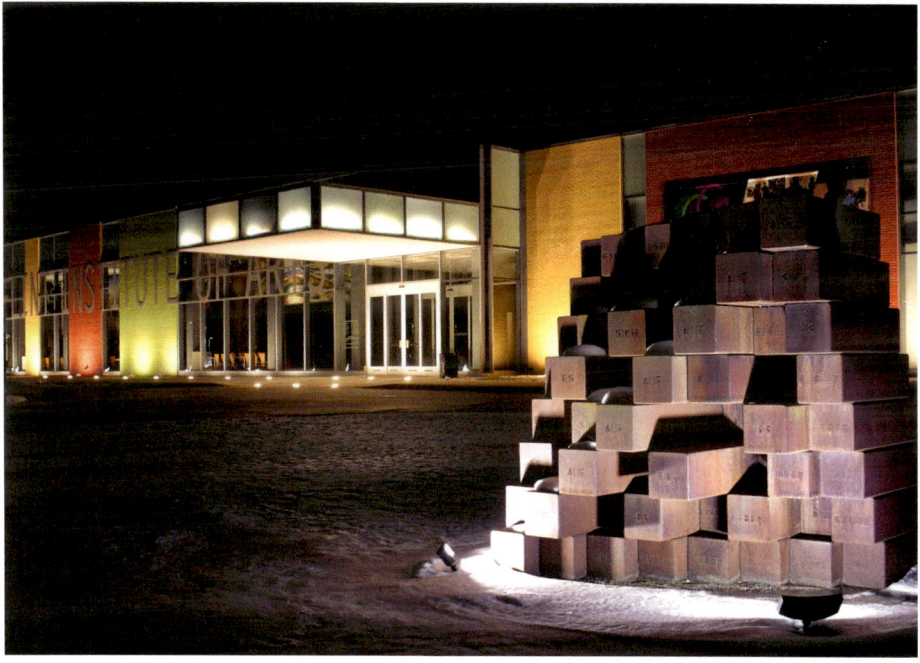

The Flint Institute of Arts shimmering with dazzling colors.

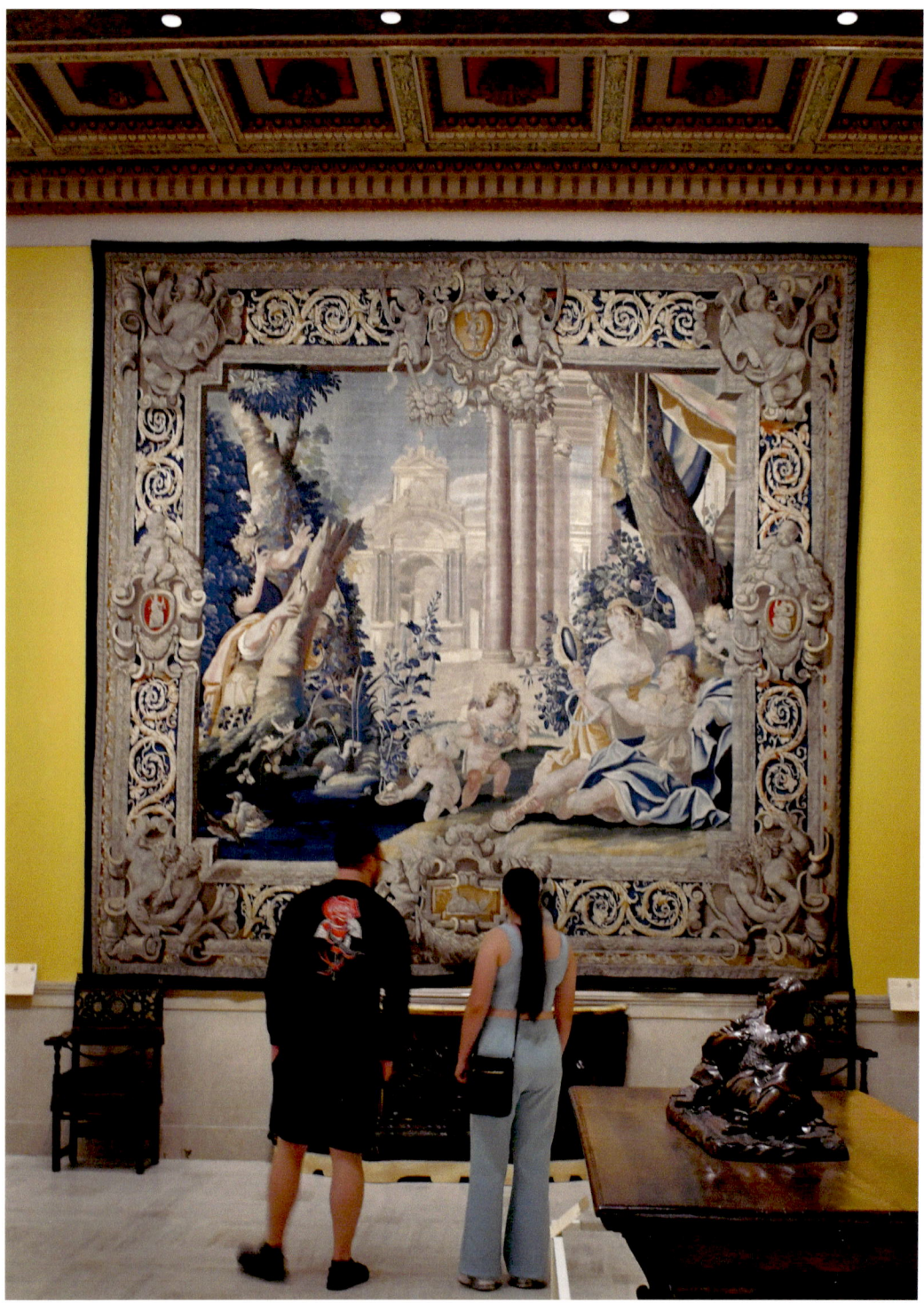

A couple admiring a vintage tapestry at the art museum in Flint.

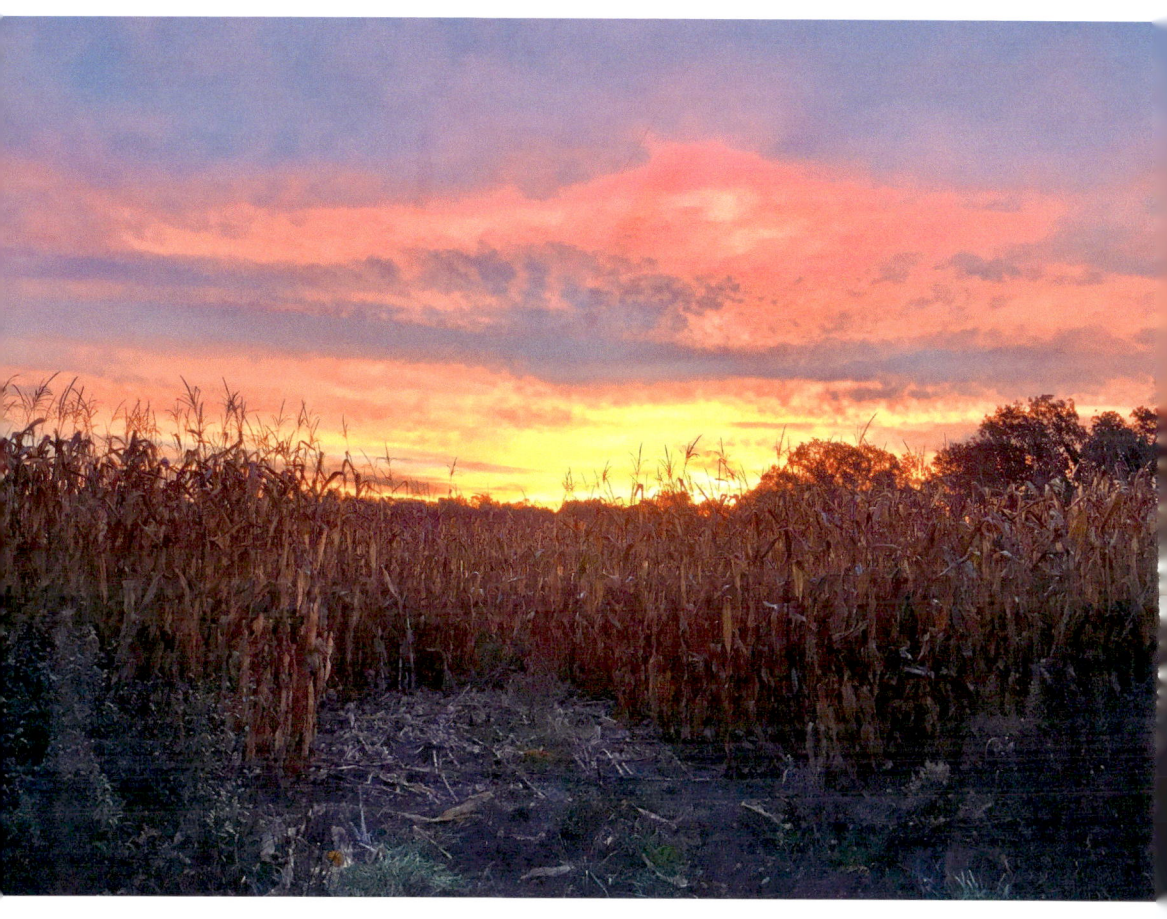

Swathes of gold-seeped rose color a sunrise over a brittle cornfield in the farmlands.

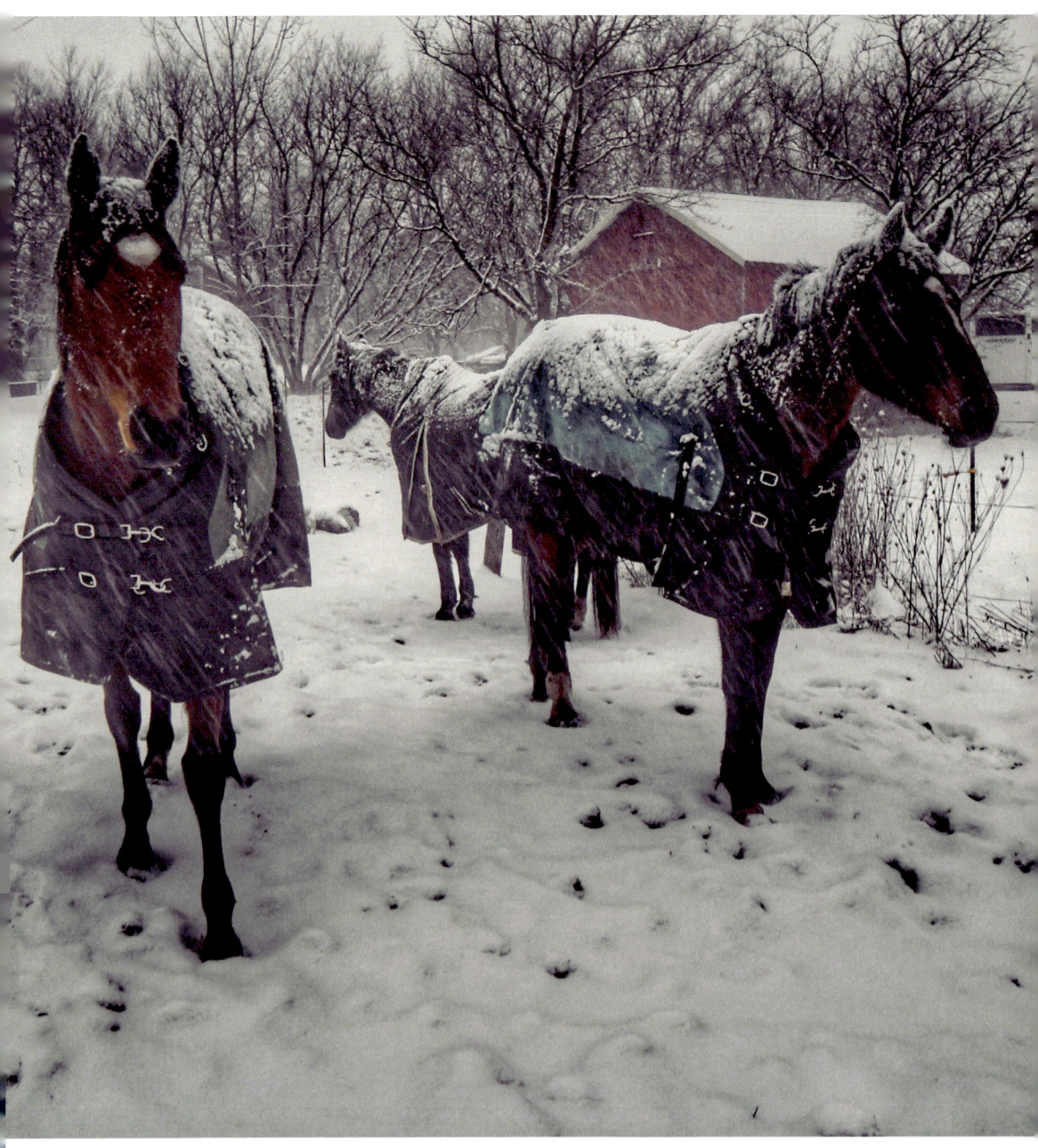

Snow-frosted horses draped in warm blankets waiting out the blizzard.